The Third Crusade 1191

Richard the Lionheart, Saladin and the
struggle for Jerusalem

Campaign • 161

The Third Crusade 1191

Richard the Lionheart, Saladin and the struggle for Jerusalem

David Nicolle · Illustrated by Christa Hook
Series editor Lee Johnson

First published in Great Britain in 2006 by Osprey Publishing, Midland House,
West Way, Botley, Oxford OX2 9LP, United Kindgom.
443 Park Avenue South, New York, NY 10016, USA
Email: info@ospreypublishing.com

A CIP catalogue record for this book is available from the British Library

ISBN 1 84176 868 5

The author, David Nicolle, has asserted his right under the Copyright, Designs
and Patents Act, 1988, to be identified as the Author of this Work.

Design: The Black Spot
Index: Sandra Shotter
Maps by The Map Studio
3d bird's-eye views by The Black Spot
Battlescene artwork by Christa Hook
Originated by The Electronic Page Company, Cwmbran, UK
Printed in China through World Print Ltd.

05 06 07 08 09   10 9 8 7 6 5 4 3 2 1

For a catalogue of all books published by Osprey please contact:

NORTH AMERICA
Osprey Direct, 2427 Bond Street, University Park, IL 60466, USA
Email: info@ospreydirect.co.uk

ALL OTHER REGIONS
Osprey Direct UK, PO Box 140, Wellinborough, Northants, NN8 2FA, UK
Email: info@ospreydirect.co.uk

www.ospreypublishing.com

Dedication

For Nadia Lotfy, a window on the EAF

Key to military symbols

XXXXX	XXXX	XXX	XX	X	III	II
Army Group	Army	Corps	Division	Brigade	Regiment	Battalion

I				Key to unit identification
Company/Battery	Infantry	Artillery	Cavalry	

Unit Identifier — Parent unit
Commander
(+) with added elements
(–) less elements

CONTENTS

ORIGINS OF THE CAMPAIGN 7

CHRONOLOGY 16

OPPOSING COMMANDERS 18
Christian commanders • Muslim commanders

OPPOSING FORCES 24
Crusader armies • Islamic forces

OPPOSING PLANS 37
King Richard's plan • Saladin's plan

THE CAMPAIGN 40
Events gather pace • The siege of Acre
The march to Arsuf • The Battle of Arsuf

AFTERMATH 83

THE BATTLEFIELD TODAY 90

BIBLIOGRAPHY 93

INDEX 95

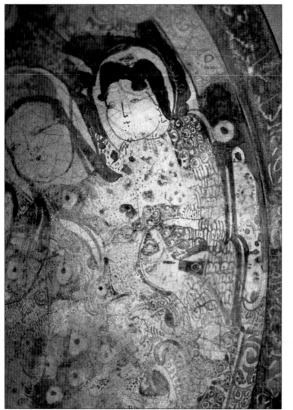

ABOVE **A copy of the wall paintings in the Templar church at Cressac, made before they were damaged during the Second World War. Here a Crusader pursues a Saracen.**

LEFT **Armoured figures are quite rare in Islamic art before the Mongols erupted into the Middle East in the 13th century. This illustration of a guardsman wearing a long lamellar cuirass is on a lustreware plate from Egypt or Iran, made in the late 12th or early 13th century. (Museum of Islamic Art, Cairo; author's photograph)**

ORIGINS OF THE CAMPAIGN

The Third Crusade was one of those events which contradicts the idea that the medieval world was characterized by major cultural blocs, such as European Christendom and the Islamic World, which had little impact upon one another. Nor was the Third Crusade an example of some supposed 'clash of civilizations' between Islam and the Christian World. It was much more complex, involving numerous competing political and cultural groups whose interests and actions did not lead to the formation of 'eastern' or 'western' blocs. Rather the Third Crusade was characterized by complex rivalries within the supposedly Christian and Islamic 'camps', which in turn resulted in unexpected and shifting alliances.

The 12th century was a period of remarkable economic and population expansion in Western Europe, accompanied by huge cultural advances and booming confidence. This process was in full flow at the time of the Third Crusade. Considerably more money was now in circulation – money which rulers and the higher aristocracy could use to hire and equip professional soldiers. This money also provided capital with which economically advanced regions such as the Italian 'naval republics' of Genoa, Pisa and Venice financed their expanding trade within and outside Europe – trade which included an arms industry which now became a boom business for manufacturers and merchants alike.

Although the Islamic World had long been in advance of Western Europe in most of these fields, the Europeans were playing 'catch up' so successfully that they overtook their Muslim rivals in several significant fields, most notably shipping and trade. Italian vessels now dominated the Mediterranean but communications within Europe were still generally slower and less efficient than in the Islamic World. Furthermore, Europeans had far inferior geographical knowledge, especially outside Europe. This geographical ignorance was more of a problem for merchants than Crusader commanders, since the latter now rarely ventured beyond territory conquered, and subsequently lost, by their predecessors. Inadequate communications were more serious, with their reliance on personal messengers or delegations which needed military protection. It also took a long time for messages to reach their destinations, and for replies to return.

While Western Europe was going through an economic revolution and a cultural renaissance, the Byzantine Empire was in relative stagnation. However, the Islamic World was also seeing

'Conrad of Monferrat arrives at Tyre' in a late 12th-century history of Genoa. This event marked the start of the Kingdom of Jerusalem's fight back against Saladin's conquests. (*Annales de Gènes,* Bib. Nat., Ms. Lat. 10136, f.108, Paris)

The military equipment used by most ordinary French and Anglo-Angevin soldiers on the Third Crusade differed little from that used during the First Crusade. Most still relied upon mail hauberks, small helmets and shields, as shown in this early 13th-century stained glass window. (Musée du Louvre, Paris; author's photograph)

significant changes. Arabic and Persian remained the languages of educated, aristocratic or 'high' society, but most political and military elites were now either Turkish in origin or Turkified in culture – even including the great Saladin who was himself of Kurdish origin.

The Western European religious, military, cultural and economic offensive typified by the Crusades had re-ignited the long dormant spirit of *jihad* within some parts of the Islamic World. The most prestigious 'primary' *jihad* to live a moral life had, of course, remained central to Islamic culture, but now the 'secondary' *jihad* or physical effort to defend Islam rose to prominence in those regions threatened by the Crusades. It was this sometimes militant secondary *jihad* – often mistranslated as Holy War – which motivated the Islamic armies of Syria, Egypt and neighbouring regions, enabling Saladin to virtually obliterate the Crusader Kingdom of Jerusalem in 1187. Seen in Latin or Catholic Christian Western Europe as a shocking reversal, Saladin's victories in turn led to the Third Crusade and the battle of Arsuf.

This revived spirit of *jihad* shifted from the defensive posture of the early and mid 12th century to an offensive strategy under Saladin. Meanwhile the Crusaders were moving from an offensive to a defensive mind-set. Given the bitter hostility between Crusader and Islamic armies during this period, it is surprising to find that Middle Eastern Muslims did not particularly hate Western Europeans. Instead they despised these 'Franks', as they called them, as culturally inferior semi-savages. Western European men were characterized as brave and strong though sexually promiscuous, while western women were considered pretty much useless for anything.

Although the westerners were somewhat in cultural awe of Moors, Arabs and Persians, though not of Turks, the Western European knightly elite was confident of the superiority of its own warriors. Nevertheless they remained cautious of perceived Byzantine and Islamic military 'cleverness'. Instead of dismissing their opponents' perceived preference for archery at a distance as a sign of cowardice, they regarded it as a result of Muslims having less blood in their veins because they lived in such hot climates.

Almost all the Islamic Middle East was ruled by Sunni Muslim elites by the late 12th century, but many areas still had Christian or Shi'a Muslim majority populations. In Damascus most Muslims were Shi'a in AD 1184 and Aleppo became a centre of Sunni scholarship while retaining a Shi'a majority. The Latin Catholic inhabitants of Jerusalem were almost entirely expelled following Saladin's reconquest and, although ten Hospitaller brethren remained to tend the sick, Saladin built a new hospital near the Church of the Holy Sepulchre, this being completed in 1192. The provision of medical and educational facilities was, of course, as much part of the struggle between competing religions as were sieges and battles. It is also likely that many of the shrines dedicated to early Muslim saints and heroes in Palestine were revived or even invented at the time of the Crusades, in order to increase the 'religious value' of the territory.

At the same time, the decline of both Shi'as and Christians reflected population movements, including those by Turks and Kurds into the largely Arab Fertile Crescent and Egypt, the Arab urban elites regarding these Turks and Kurds as near barbarians – though at least they were Muslims. Political and religious oppression did exist, but was usually at a low level. Otherwise, most non-Sunni populations were left alone, though they were increasingly excluded from the upper ranks of political, military and cultural life. Another little-known aspect of life in the Middle East at this time concerned drug-taking. The use of hashish and henbane, both of which were called *banj*, now spread amongst ordinary people. Hashish was even permitted by the Hanafi school of Islamic law and would become very cheap during the 13th century.

In strategic and military terms, the Crusader States were left virtually on their own following the death of the Byzantine Emperor Manuel in 1180, and an alliance with the Byzantines – always difficult – became almost impossible. Active support from Western Europe was also fitful and unreliable until the shock of the fall of Jerusalem suddenly revived enthusiasm for crusading. Meanwhile, the Crusader States were torn between the need to co-exist with their Muslim neighbours, and a continuing cultural drive to convert or defeat them. They were also

Saladin held large numbers of prisoners taken during his conquest of almost all of the Kingdom of Jerusalem before the Third Crusade. Some may even have been incarcerated in the so-called dungeons – actually storerooms – within the Citadel of Aleppo. (Author's photograph)

changing from land-based feudal societies, attempting to emulate the French model, to urbanized coastal enclaves reflecting Italian rather than French cultural priorities.

The population of the Crusader Kingdom of Jerusalem before the catastrophe of 1187 was around 100,000–120,000 largely urban 'Franks' or people of Western European origin and Latin Catholic religion, plus 300,000–360,000 indigenous Christians and Muslims of whom two-thirds lived in the countryside. There are also said to have been up to 20,000 Muslim slaves, the majority of whom were freed as a result of Saladin's reconquests. The fate of the 'Frankish' settler population is very unclear. Battlefield casualties only affected a section of society and those who escaped capture presumably crowded into what remained of Crusader territory. For the Kingdom of Jerusalem this meant the coastal city of Tyre. To the north the County of Tripoli and the Principality of Antioch were also reduced in size, so there must have been widespread destitution, social collapse and economic chaos.

In political terms, the disasters of 1187–88 deepened the rifts amongst the barons of the Crusader States. Most of those who had been antagonistic to King Guy, regarding him as a usurper, now believed that the Kingdom of Jerusalem had been defeated because their advice was ignored. One was Renaud of Sidon, a strong supporter of Count Raymond of Tripoli, who had survived the battle of Hattin. He fled to Tyre and tried to save what was left, assisted by a fleet which arrived from the Norman Kingdom of Sicily, but, like other surviving members of the local aristocracy and church leaders, Renaud then opened negotiations with Saladin. At this point Conrad of Monferrat unexpectedly arrived from Constantinople and convinced the people of Tyre to break off discussions. The Sicilian fleet withdrew, but was replaced by a Pisan fleet in 1188. It may have been Conrad's background in northern Italy which led him to encourage the formation of an urban commune, uniting all available forces in a common cause, this having been a typical feature of northern Italy in the 12th century.

This dramatic moment could be seen as the start of the Third Crusade. Renaud's own coastal city of Sidon fell during the first rush of Saladin's conquests, but the inland castle of Beaufort held out and it was here that Renaud of Sidon now took up position. What followed was a long period of siege and negotiation during which Renaud offered, perhaps as a ploy to prolong the talking, to surrender in return for a refuge and a pension in Damascus. By then, of course, things were afoot in Europe.

Saladin's failure to take Tyre has been seen by many historians as a monumental error. In reality he was following accepted strategic principals within his own military culture. These advised a ruler to maintain the momentum of success, mop up easy targets, avoid setbacks which could undermine his prestige, while isolating the enemy's principal strongholds. Unfortunately this strategy had one major flaw. Islamic navies no longer dominated the eastern Mediterranean, so Saladin could not 'isolate' coastal enclaves like Tyre which could maintain contact with Western Europe by sea – at least while navigation was 'open' from March

Knights and foot soldiers burst into a city while defenders resist from the gate towers, in an English manuscript made around the time of the Third Crusade. (*The Great Canterbury Psalter*, Bib. Nat., Ms. Lat. 8846, Paris)

to October. Saladin was aware of this limitation and put great effort into reviving his fleet.

Instead Saladin's army campaigned further north, focusing on the already reduced Principality of Antioch where, as Arab chroniclers wrote of Antioch itself, 'To take away her castles is to take away her life.' In fact, the principality survived many more years because Saladin faced huge logistical and communications problems caused by the mountains and main roads running north–south, separating the Mediterranean ports from Saladin's power bases in the great Arab–Islamic cities of the interior. Nevertheless, by the end of 1188, Saladin largely succeeded in cutting off the narrow land route from the Crusader Kingdom of Jerusalem to Europe.

The Crusader States were not the only matters which Saladin had to consider. After overthrowing the Shi'a Muslim Fatimid Caliphate in Egypt, Saladin inherited the Fatimids' generally good relations with the Byzantine Empire. This reflected a strategic imperative which long predated the Fatimids and long outlasted Saladin. To the south, Saladin re-established stable relations with the Christian Nubian states of northern Sudan, which had previously been strong allies of the Fatimids, and there is no evidence of strategic co-operation between the Crusader States and Christian Nubia within the Red Sea region. Saladin's own interests in the Red Sea were, however, clear. This was a highly lucrative trade route and Saladin's decision to conquer Yemen was primarily to ensure Egyptian domination over the sea route to the Indian Ocean. On the other hand, Yemen was too far away and militarily too backward to contribute anything directly towards Saladin's struggle with the Crusaders.

At another far frontier of his empire in the Jazira region, in what are now northern Iraq, north-east Syria and south-eastern Turkey, Saladin faced other difficulties. This was a rich, fertile, urbanized and densely populated area with a long tradition of warfare against the Byzantine Empire. It was also politically fragmented and ethnically mixed with long-established Armenian, Kurdish and Arab populations to which a now militarily and politically dominant Turkish element had been added since the mid 11th century. Consequently the Jazira (literally the 'island' between the Euphrates and Tigris rivers, the Mesopotamia 'between the rivers' of ancient times) was a source of political problems as well as numerous, skilful and warlike troops.

Amongst the rival local dynasties were the Zangids, descended from Imad al-Din Zangi, the Turkish warrior who had first rolled back the Crusader conquests. They, their supporters and the *Atabegs* ('guiding fathers'), who sometimes held real power, regarded themselves as more legitimate rulers than the upstart Kurd, Saladin. Then there was the Turkish Artuqid dynasty, descended from conquerors who entered the

Saladin had the great fortress of Qalaat al-Gindi built to defend a strategic pass in western Sinai. After the battle of Arsuf there was widespread concern that King Richard's Crusader army would threaten Egypt. (Author's photograph)

region with the Saljuq Great Sultans back in the 11th century. They also tended to see themselves as superior to Saladin. Most of these highly cultured rulers lived in urban citadels in the midst of mixed Armenian, Arab or other urban communities, while the bulk of the Turkoman tribes who formed their powerbase lived outside, either wholly or partially nomadic. The rural Armenian, Arab and Kurdish populations again varied from valley to valley, while there were also tensions between nomads, settled peasantry, and urban populations.

To control his recently conquered and in many areas merely politically dominated empire, Saladin relied on a remarkably effective administration and army. The former was based upon a centuries-old tradition to which Saladin added his own system of patronage. Unfortunately, Saladin's military commanders did not always show themselves to be good at civilian administration, nor were they necessarily keen to accept the expensive role of governing a province or even a castle. Indeed Saladin himself was probably campaigning beyond his financial means, and needed victories to pay or equip his troops. This problem would re-emerge during Saladin's struggle against the Third Crusade.

Before looking at the situation in Western Europe, some political and military developments within the Byzantine Empire need to be noted. The Empire, currently ruled by Emperor Isaac Angelus, was in economic and military decline, though probably not in a state of economic collapse as is sometimes claimed. Things were reasonably stable on the Anatolian frontier, where the previous Comnenid dynasty had pushed deep inland from the Aegean coast and had largely confined the Saljuq Turkish Sultanate of Rum to the central plateau. In the Balkans, however, the Byzantine Empire was in deep trouble. The Pecheneg Turks who had been forced south of the river Danube in the mid 11th century by more powerful Kipchaq Turks behind them, were largely integrated into the Byzantine military system. Other Pechenegs retreated into Hungary while another Turkish group, the Ouzes, seem to have been forced into the southern Carpathian mountains, perhaps merging with the existing Vlachs whose Latin-based language (Romanian) dated back to Roman times.

The situation was very complex, with historians still arguing bitterly over the extent of real Byzantine control in the mid 1180s. What is clear is that the Byzantine Empire was already having trouble controlling what is now northern Bulgaria where a new independent Bulgarian state would soon emerge. For the moment, however, the Kipchaq Turks and indigenous Vlachs in Wallachia (southern Romania) seem to have made common cause against the Byzantines. Twentieth-century Romanian and Bulgarian historians disagreed vehemently over who dominated the 1186 revolt in the Balkan range – Bulgars, Vlachs or Kipchaqs. But for the German Emperor Frederick Barbarossa and his Crusader army the main fact was that Byzantine regional authority was fast falling apart (see below). Further west, Serbia was in reality already independent, though nominally accepting Byzantine suzerainty, while down on the Adriatic coast the collapse of Byzantine authority around AD 1180 changed the whole balance of power in the Adriatic. All these considerations would have an impact on Crusader contingents travelling overland to Palestine, and even on those sailing from Venice down the Adriatic Sea.

TOP **Saladin as a Byzantine-style ruler on a copper coin from Nisibin, minted in AD 1182–83.**

BOTTOM **Saladin as a Turkish-style ruler on a copper coin from northern Iraq, minted in AD 1190–91.**

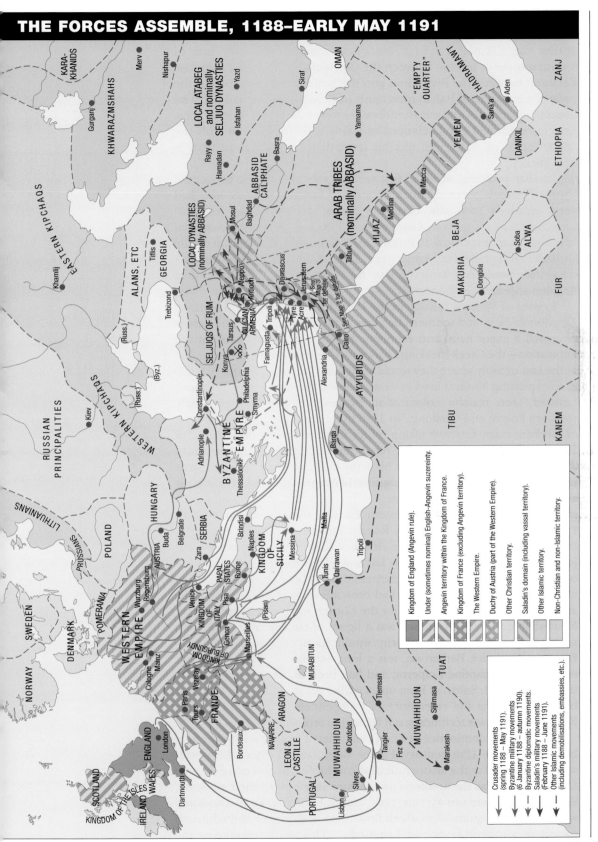

Kingdom of England (Angevin rule).

Under (sometimes nominal) English-Angevin suzereinty.

Angevin territory within the Kingdom of France.

Kingdom of France (excluding Angevin territory).

The Western Empire.

Duchy of Austria (part of the Western Empire).

Other Christian territory.

Saladin's domain (including vassal territory).

Other Islamic territory.

Non-Christian and non-Islamic territory.

Crusader movements
(spring 1188 – May 1191).

Byzantine military movements
(6 January 1188 – autumn 1190).

Byzantine diplomatic movements.

Saladin's military movements
(February 1188 – June 1191).

Other Islamic movements
(including demobilisations, embassies, etc.).

A previous Byzantine Emperor, Manuel Comnenus (1143–80), had supported the northern Italian city states in their struggle for autonomy against the German Emperor Frederick, and this was only one of several sources of tension between the German and Byzantine Empires. Relations between the Byzantines and the Italians then slumped in the wake of a massacre of Italian merchants in Constantinople in 1182. The Byzantines were not entirely friendless, however, and the Emperor Isaac Angelus cultivated good relations not only with Saladin but with the Saljuq Sultan of Rum who was his immediate neighbour in what is now Turkey.

Another problem, which at first seemed relatively minor, concerned Cyprus. This was currently ruled by a rebel, Isaac Comnenus, who had good relations with the Crusader States. Indeed Isaac Angelus' unsuccessful attack on Isaac Comnenus in 1187 was seen in the Kingdom of Jerusalem as tantamount to support for Saladin during his assault on the Crusader Kingdom that same year. Isaac Comnenus' pro-Crusader credentials would not, however, save his regime once King Richard of England appeared on the scene.

So what of Western Europe in the late 1180s? The powerful Norman Kingdom in Sicily and southern Italy was in political crisis. Nevertheless, it remained a major naval and economic power with a remarkably mixed population – the Greek-speaking Orthodox Christians being concentrated in the east of Sicily where they would soon clash with the Crusaders, while Arabic-speaking Muslims lived in western Sicily. Twelfth-century Sicily had, however, seen massive colonization by people from northern Italy, southern France and Catalonia. In 1190 there was a widespread massacre of Muslims, many survivors taking refuge in the mountainous interior of Sicily which would remain under rebel domination for many years. Like the Emperor Frederick as he led his army into Byzantine territory, kings Richard of England and Philip Augustus of France would soon lead their armies into a volatile environment.

Like many other parts of Western Europe, the German or Western Empire, later known as the Holy Roman Empire, was in the midst of a cultural and economic renaissance. Amongst those who benefited were the Jews who were better protected by law and by the Emperor than in most other Christian countries. To some extent this was because of the appalling massacres of German Jews which had been a feature of the First Crusade, and which neither the Emperor nor the Church wanted to happen again. Meanwhile the Emperor himself was a figure of considerable power and prestige, though his real authority would soon decline. The current Emperor, Frederick Barbarossa, was a long-established rival if not overt enemy of the Byzantine Emperor, and had been in communication with the Saljuq Turkish Sultan of Rum on an earlier occasion. He may also have been encouraging the emergence of independent principalities in the Balkans, in what was technically still Byzantine territory.

The political dominance of France only dated from the 13th century, but, even in the 12th century, France dominated Western European secular culture. For the aristocratic and knightly elites of most of Europe *la douce France* was the aesthetic and fashionable hub of their universe. Yet even here there was an emerging 'cultural underground' associated with dualistic religious ideas which flourished in the open and educated society of southern France or Languedoc. This would emerge as the

Cathar heresy of the early 13th century, which in turn prompted the savage Albigensian Crusades.

Meanwhile, the throne of France was occupied by one of the most successful kings in French history. Philip Augustus was born in 1165 and was known in medieval French chronicles as Philippe-Dieudonné, 'the gift from heaven'. He continued the work of his father, Louis VII, reviving the wealth, power and authority of the monarchy. Shrewd, calculating, and with a highly dubious private life, King Philip Augustus had, by the time of his death in 1223, overcome internal foes, defeated external ones, and virtually evicted his Angevin rivals from the soil of France.

The Angevins, better known in English history as the Plantagenets, were descended from the Counts of Anjou. The first Angevin king of England was Henry II, who was succeeded by his sons Richard I and John. They in turn inherited not only the crown of England and political suzerainty over almost the entire British Isles, but also more than half of the territory of France. These vast French lands they held as French barons under the suzerainty of the French king. In most other respects, however, the Angevin rulers of England were more powerful and certainly richer than their rivals in Paris. In cultural terms the Angevin kings of England were also French rather than English, which was still also true of most of their aristocratic followers, even in England.

This superb ceramic horseman was found at al-Rafiqa, a ruined palace near Raqqa. It was made in Syria during the 12th century. (National Museum, Damascus; author's photograph)

CHRONOLOGY

1187

14 July Conrad of Monferrat arrives in Tyre which ends surrender negotiations with Saladin.

November Richard of Poitou (future King Richard I) takes the cross.

1188

January King Henry II of England and King Philip Augustus of France take the cross.

6 January Embassy from the Byzantine Emperor Isaac II Angelus congratulates Saladin on his liberation of Jerusalem.

March The German Emperor Frederick takes the cross; Saladin inspects the siege of Belvoir.

Spring King William II of Sicily sends a fleet to support Tyre, Tripoli and Antioch.

May Crusading fleets set sail from northern Europe.

1 July Finding Tripoli too strong to be besieged, Saladin begins a campaign to take Crusader castles in northern Syria.

3 September Crusading fleets from northern Europe help the Portuguese conquer Silves.

1 October Saladin agrees an eight-month truce with Prince Bohemond III of Antioch.

Winter 1188–89 Saladin takes the Crusader castles of Safad and Belvoir.

1189

Spring Saladin besieges Beaufort.

May Emperor Frederick sets out at the head of a huge crusading army.

3–13 June Crusader troops from Tyre advance against Sidon but are forced back.

6 July Henry II dies; Richard becomes King of England.

Summer Pisan fleet reaches the eastern Mediterranean in support of Tyre.

August Serbian and Bulgarian representatives offer to form an anti-Byzantine alliance with Emperor Frederick during his stay at Nish, but Frederick does not accept.

28 August King Guy 'of Jerusalem' arrives with a small force from Tyre, supported by the Pisan fleet, to besiege Saladin's garrison in Acre.

August–November Emperor Frederick occupies Plovdiv; Emperor Isaac seizes Emperor Frederick's representatives as hostages; Isaac agrees to transport Frederick's army across the Dardanelles.

15 September Saladin moves against King Guy outside Acre, besieging the Crusader force which is besieging Acre.

Autumn Crusader contingents from Cologne, Frisia, Bremen and Thuringia take the sea route from Venice to the siege of Acre.

4 October Saladin defeats a Crusader assault on Acre but a Crusader counterattack pursues some of Saladin's troops as far as al-'Ayadiya.

16 October Saladin's forces pull back to al-Kharruba.

October, late Egyptian fleet brings supplies and troops to Acre.

November King William II of Sicily dies; his successor Queen Constance is unacceptable and is replaced by Tancred of Lecce.

1190

March Emperor Frederick crosses into Anatolia.

Spring Contingents from northern Syria are sent to guard the frontier against Emperor Frederick.

27 April–5 May Prolonged Crusader attack on Acre fails.

17 May A Seljuq army attempts but fails to stop Emperor Frederick entering Konya.

10 June Emperor Frederick drowns in the river Göksu.

July King Richard and King Philip Augustus lead their crusading armies from Vézelay; Beaufort surrenders to Saladin's troops.

Summer Count Henry of Champagne and his contingent join the siege of Acre.

22 August King Richard's fleet from England and France arrives in Marseilles, but finds that Richard has already left.

September, mid King Philip Augustus and his crusading army land in Sicily.

16 September Richard's advance force under Archbishop Baldwin reaches Tyre.

22 September King Richard arrives in Messina.

October–November Outside Acre, contingents from northern Iraq demand to go home; Saladin agrees.

Winter 1190–91 Richard and Philip Augustus winter in Sicily amid increasing acrimony; Duke Leopold of Austria's Crusader army winters in Zara having sailed from Venice.

1191

18 January Embassy from Saladin asks the Muwahhid Caliph Ya'qub al-Mansur for naval support, but this is refused.

13 February Saladin's troops break through the siege lines into Acre with a relief army and new commander.

30 March Philip Augustus leaves Sicily for Tyre.

Spring, early Leopold of Austria rallies the remnants of Emperor Frederick's Crusade in Acre.

Spring Taqi al-Din and the governor of Diyar Bakr do not respond to Saladin's summons for reinforcements because they are competing for domination in the same region.

10 April Richard leaves Sicily for the Holy Land via Crete and Rhodes.

1 May Richard reaches Rhodes.

12 May Richard and his army land in Cyprus and defeat Isaac Comnenus' troops.

20 May Philip Augustus and his army join the siege of Acre.

31 May Isaac Comnenus surrenders to Richard at Kantara.

5 June French attack Acre but pull back when Saladin attacks their siege lines.

June Richard and his army join the siege of Acre.

June, mid Genoese fleet arrives to strengthen blockade of Acre.

June, late French attack Acre but Richard refuses to take part.

3 July French again attack Acre and breach the fortifications.

July Garrison of Acre sends delegation to Crusader camp to discuss terms; Saladin is shocked to hear the garrison is considering surrender.

July Richard's troops attack the ruined Maledicta Tower of Acre.

July Swimmer brings desperate plea to Saladin from garrison, saying they cannot hold out any longer.

1 July English and Pisan troops again attack the ruined Maledicta Tower; Saladin makes a final attempt to break the siege.

2 July Garrison of Acre surrenders without Saladin's authority.

4 July Saladin organizes the collection of ransom money and Crusader prisoners for release.

7–28 July Council of Crusader leaders decides to divide the Kingdom of Jerusalem with King Guy controlling Acre and the south, while Conrad of Monferrat controls Tyre and the north.

1 July Philip Augustus and Conrad of Monferrat leave Acre for Tyre.

August Philip Augustus leaves Tyre for France.

0 August Following disputes about the payment of ransoms and the release of prisoners, Richard orders the massacre of the prisoners and their families.

4 August Part of Saladin's army moves to Caymont.

5 August The Crusader army sets off in three divisions, following the coast; the Crusader fleet accompanies offshore.

5–26 August King Richard's contingent moves ahead to seize Merle; al-Afdal attacks the Crusader rearguard; Saladin sends his baggage train towards Majdal Yaba; al-Adil's corps heads for the coast; other contingents remain at Caymont or are sent to observe the Crusader army; Saladin makes a reconnaissance of the coast.

7–28 August Saladin orders his baggage train to return; Crusader army makes a short march because the fleet is delayed rounding Mount Carmel.

9 August Crusader army remains encamped.

0 August Crusader army advances towards Caesarea, with fleet offshore; Muslim attacks have little effect; Crusaders make camp at the Nahr al-Zarqa.

4 August Crusaders remain in camp.

September Crusaders march past Caesarea to the Nahr al-Mafjir.

September Crusaders march to Nahr al-Qasab despite intensive Muslim attacks.

September Saladin's army moves to the Forest of Arsuf; the Crusaders remain in camp.

September Crusaders march to the Nahr al-Falik; King Richard contacts al-Adil for talks; Saladin sends his baggage train south then orders it to return.

September Crusaders do not move; Saladin's baggage train sent off again.

September Battle of Arsuf; Crusaders camp near Arsuf.

September Saladin's army moves south.

September Crusaders march within a few kilometres of Jaffa; Saladin prepared to break off contact; Crusaders remain in Jaffa until 31 October.

0–11 September Saladin pulls back to Ramla; Saladin goes to Ascalon to supervise the demolition of its fortifications and the moving of its population to Syria and Egypt.

23–24 September Saladin returns to Ramla and then inspects the defences of Jerusalem; al-Afdal remains in Ascalon.

17 October Richard meets al-Adil's clerk and requests negotiations; negotiations continue on and off for the remainder of the Third Crusade.

October, late Envoys from Conrad of Monferrat in Tyre to al-Adil at Lydda; from October onwards the Crusaders remain in Jaffa, few skirmishes on plain of Lydda; increasing dissension within the Crusader army.

17–22 November Saladin pulls back to Latrun; Crusaders occupy Ramla; skirmishing continues.

12 December Saladin disbands most of his army and withdraws to Jerusalem.

25 December Crusader advance guard reaches Bayt Nuba.

28–29 December Richard renews advance into hills; Muslim unit under Sabiq al-Din 'Uthman attacks Crusader outposts.

1192

3 January Richard reaches Bayt Nuba.

8 January Richard orders retreat to Ramla.

20 January Crusader Council at Ramla agrees that Richard lead army to Ascalon; Crusaders remain there until 6 June, rebuilding fortifications.

February Al-Afdal leaves Jerusalem for Syria; fighting in Acre between pro-King Guy Pisans and pro-Conrad of Monferrat Genoese.

20 February Richard arrives in Acre and tries to make peace; Richard also requests a meeting with al-Adil.

20 March Al-Adil goes to Richard's camp with a peace offer.

April, early Richard summons Crusader leaders and demands that the question of the crown of Jerusalem be settled but is surprised when all want Conrad to replace Guy as king.

28 April Conrad of Monferrat assassinated in Tyre.

5 May Marriage of Henry of Champagne and Isabella in Acre, followed by coronation as King and Queen of Jerusalem.

18–23 May Richard and the Crusader army attack Darum by land and sea.

9–11 June Richard and Crusader army make camp east of Latrun; Saladin prepares to defend Jerusalem; skirmishing between Muslim and Crusader troops.

22–23 June Richard takes a large force and attacks caravan in Wadi al-Hasi.

1–3 July Saladin holds council in Jerusalem to discuss whether to remain or retreat eastward; Saladin assumes command of field army outside Jerusalem.

4 July Crusaders abandon Bayt Nuba and retreat towards Ramla.

9–19 July Richard requests negotiations; Saladin breaks off negotiations because Richard refuses to demolish Ascalon.

27–31 July Absence of Richard enables Saladin to take town of Jaffa but Citadel holds out; Richard returns by sea with Pisans and Genoese and retakes Jaffa.

4 August Saladin unsuccessfully attacks Crusaders outside Jaffa.

20 August Negotiations resume.

1–3 September Peace terms are agreed and signed by both sides.

9 October Richard sails homeward from Acre.

15 October Saladin meets Prince Bohemond of Antioch in Beirut.

4 November Saladin returns to Damascus.

OPPOSING COMMANDERS

CHRISTIAN COMMANDERS

The Third Crusade began, like all previous multinational crusades, with a divided command. But, after the Emperor Frederick Barbarossa of Germany died in southern Turkey and King Philip Augustus of France returned home after the successful siege of Acre, only one top-ranking leader remained: **King Richard I of England**, known as *Coeur de Lion*. Born in 1157, Richard learned the arts of administration and war as governor of the Angevin fiefdom of Aquitaine which included most of western France south of the Loire. Richard of Poitou, as he was often known, was not a dutiful son, rebelling against his father King Henry II between 1173 and 1174 and again in 1189. That same year Henry II died and Richard became King of England.

Richard's motivation, as well as his sexuality, have been the subject of academic debate, and like Philip Augustus of France he used crusading to enhance his own reputation. In fact Richard 'took the cross', publicly declaring his intention of going on crusade, before his father died and this decision earned him widespread respect within his own realms. On the other hand it would be misleading to see Richard's crusade merely as a political ploy or a warlike adventure. As the historian D. Carpenter recently wrote: 'For someone often prey to a morbid sense of his own sinfulness, the spiritual benefits of the crusade, with the promise of remission of all sins, were compelling. So was the chance to exercise martial talents... not against fellow Christians but against the infidels.'[1] Richard's remarkable achievement on the Third Crusade was also summed up by Matthew Bennett, a respected medieval military historian: 'Richard managed to weld together the disparate forces of the Third Crusade under his authority because of his charisma and evident knowledge of warfare. The Crusaders of 1191–92 had forged common links outside the walls of Acre which overrode most of their divisions. More identifiably belonging to separate nations than a century earlier, they were also capable of transcending that loyalty for the immediate cause.'[2]

Duke Hugues III of Burgundy (1162–91) was a cousin of **King Philip Augustus of France** and was married to one the King's sisters. Having travelled to the Holy Land with Philip Augustus, Duke Hugues played a major role during the siege of Acre. There, like several other leaders, he paid for the building and operation of one of the huge stone-throwing mangonels which battered the city walls. Given his status within the ruling elite, it is not surprising that he was

The second Great Seal of King Richard I of England. (Public Records Office, London)

18

nominated as commander of French forces after King Philip Augustus returned to France. Philip would, in fact, leave most of his fighting men in Palestine, plus 5,000 marks in gold and silver to pay them.

During the first stages of the Crusaders' march south from Acre, Hugues and the French formed the rearguard, bearing the brunt of a determined attack by Saladin on 30 August when Hugues of Burgundy demonstrated considerable capability as a field commander. He was subsequently co-commander of the whole Crusader army at the battle of Arsuf, but relations between the French and Angevin contingents were already deteriorating with the quarrel between Hugues and Richard soon becoming public. The Duke of Burgundy's money also ran out and he had to borrow from Richard to pay his troops. After Richard abandoned the Crusader advance towards Jerusalem, Hugues withdrew his men in disgust, after which Richard not surprisingly stopped paying them. The English also accused Hugues of Burgundy of composing a rude song about King Richard, to which the English king responded with a rival song. Duke Hugues III of Burgundy died in Acre shortly before peace was concluded and King Richard, who was also ill, is said to have started feeling better as soon as he heard the news.

Another French nobleman who took a leading role in the Third Crusade was **Henry III, Count of Troyes** and a leading member of the powerful house of Champagne. His predecessors Counts Henry I and Henry II also fought in the Holy Land. He himself arrived in what remained of the Kingdom of Jerusalem during the summer of 1190, long before Richard or Philip Augustus. There **Henry of Champagne** was placed in command of the siege and is said to have spent no less than 1,500 dinars on the construction of just one great stone-throwing mangonel as well as some formidable battering rams. Henry of Champagne remained in command until King Philip and King Richard arrived in 1191. During the battle of Arsuf he commanded both the infantry and the baggage train.

Though he was a nephew of both Richard and Philip Augustus, Henry of Champagne chose to be a close political ally of Richard. When it became clear that nobody wanted Guy as King of Jerusalem, and, after his nominated successor Conrad of Monferrat was assassinated, Henry of Champagne was selected as the best remaining candidate; but to become King he had to wed Conrad's widow, Isabella, for whom it would be her third marriage. Though it was a political match, the wedding seemed happy enough and, as the chronicler Ambroise wrote:

> The French delayed not in the least
> > But sent straightway to fetch the priest
> And caused the Count to wed the Dame.
> > My soul, I should have done the same,
> For she was fair and beautiful
> > And, may God be merciful
> To me, the Count, unless I ere,
> > Was well disposed to marry her.

Henry of Champagne never adopted the title 'King of Jerusalem' and he was often known as King of the Coast. However, he remained ruler of what remained of the Kingdom until 1197 when he stepped backwards out of a window and was killed. Isabella then married her fourth and final husband, who died eight years later after eating too much fish. Isabella was still only 33 years old but had earned a reputation as a dangerous woman to wed.

The position of **King Guy of Jerusalem** was not a happy one during the Third Crusade. Before the catastrophes of 1187, he had been widely regarded as too easily influenced by his friends and of being indecisive. Many powerful barons also regarded him as a usurper and he was widely blamed for the loss of Jerusalem. On the other hand it was Guy who took the daring decision to lead a small army from the relative security of Tyre to besiege Acre in 1189. During the course of the Crusade, Guy failed to improve his standing and he never had more than a nominal command position. At Arsuf he was in charge of the men of Poitou and Guienne, but even here he shared command with his brother Geoffrey de Lusignan, while the knights of the Kingdom of Jerusalem were led by James d'Avesnes.

MUSLIM COMMANDERS

The command structure of most medieval Islamic armies was more straightforward than that of their Crusader opponents because there was usually one overall commander. **Al-Malik al-Nasir Yusuf Ibn Najm al-Din Ayyub Ibn Shahdi Abu'l-Muzaffar Salah al-Din** – or Saladin as he is more commonly known – is widely regarded as the greatest hero of the Crusades, even in Europe. Most chroniclers present him as a man of outstanding virtue, courage and political skill, although recently efforts have been made to portray Saladin as an ambitious, ruthless and even devious politician, and as a less than brilliant commander.

His family, which became known as the Ayyubids, was of Kurdish origin but was Arabized in culture and Turkified in political outlook. They served Nur al-Din, the Turkish ruler of Syria, northern Iraq and Egypt, during the second half of the 12th century. Saladin himself was educated and given military training in Nur al-Din's court but it was in Egypt that Saladin rose to prominence. Saladin clearly listened to political advice and in military matters he made full use of both established and new ideas. As a military commander Saladin succeeded in keeping large and disparate forces in the field for long periods, but even he could not maintain a large volunteer army through the winter months. He already had experience as a staff officer under Nur al-Din and took part in several battles before becoming the real, though not yet official, ruler of Egypt in 1169. Only after Nur al-Din's death in 1173 did Saladin set about dominating the rest of what had been his realm.

In military matters Saladin was clearly willing to take calculated risks and his clear understanding of broad strategic issues was superior to that of most of his Crusader foes. Nevertheless, some of his decisions appear to have been wrong, at least with the benefit of hindsight, although Saladin, by allowing Crusader

Medieval Islamic civilization did not idealize its warrior aristocracy as European civilization did. Here, in a ceramic dish from Iran, a typical late 12th- or early 13th-century portrayal of a Muslim prince shown with a glass in his hand and talking to a princess. (Reza Abbasi Museum, Tehran; author's photograph)

Representations of elite guardsmen were popular in early Islamic art. They were usually shown carrying sheathed swords in front of their bodies. This example is on a 12th-century carved marble basin from Egypt. (Museum of Islamic Art, Cairo; author's photograph)

resistance to crystallize at Tyre after his overwhelming victory at Hattin, was acting within established medieval Islamic military thinking. The battle of Arsuf could be seen in the same light. Both may, in fact, indicate that Saladin was a competent rather than innovative commander, and a better leader than he was a general.

Al-Malik al-Adil Abu Bakr Muhammad Ibn Ayyub Sayf al-Din, known to the Crusaders as Saphadin, was one of Saladin's brothers, chief assistant and his philosophical as well as political heir. Born in Damascus or Baalbek between 1143 and 1145, al-Adil accompanied Saladin to Egypt in 1169. His first important official appointment was as governor of Egypt while Saladin campaigned in Syria. In this role al-Adil was highly capable, utterly loyal and was consequently allowed almost completely independent authority within Egypt. Indeed, some Arab chroniclers described al-Adil as Sultan of Egypt even during Saladin's lifetime. After a period as governor of Aleppo in Syria, al-Adil was transferred back to Egypt, this time as regent for Saladin's young son al-Aziz. He remained in this position during the campaigns that retook Jerusalem and throughout the Third Crusade when, in addition to sending troops and ships, al-Adil occasionally fought at the head of his own Egyptian contingent. It also seems that it was al-Adil who saved the day at the battle of Arsuf.

When Saladin died in 1193, al-Adil had to stop the *Atabeg* of Mosul from taking advantage of the situation and seizing the Jazira region. He then tried to mediate in the bitter rivalries between Saladin's sons, but eventually turned against Saladin's eldest son al-Afdal, defeated him and was proclaimed Sultan of both Egypt and Syria. Thereafter, until his death in 1218, al-Adil proved to be one of the most effective rulers in the Ayyubid dynasty founded by Saladin – in some ways greater than Saladin himself.

Al-Malik al-Afdal 'Ali Ibn al-Nasir Yusuf was the eldest of Saladin's 17 sons. Normally known simply as al-Afdal, the youngster accompanied his father to Egypt in 1177 when he was only seven. Brought up to be a ruler and military leader, he was made nominal governor of Egypt under the guidance of Saladin's nephew **Taqi al-Din**. There was soon friction between the two and around 1186, Taqi al-Din complained to Saladin that he could neither oppose al-Afdal's wishes nor govern Egypt properly. The youngster wanted greater independence and was developing a reputation for obstinacy as well as self-indulgence. Even Saladin himself became aware of al-Afdal's arrogance, impatience and premature ambition.

The story of how the seventeen-year-old al-Afdal became overconfident, then downcast, then overexcited at the battle of Hattin is well known. Four years later, at the battle of Arsuf he showed himself unduly emotional and prone to panic. Al-Afdal was later made governor of Damascus which he ruled from 1186 to 1196, while his younger brother **al-Aziz** was made governor of Egypt. This may reflect Saladin's assessment of his two eldest sons, because it would have been more normal for Egypt to go to the senior of the two. Rivalry between al-Afdal of Damascus and al-Aziz of Egypt almost tore the state apart after Saladin's death. At first al-Adil, as the family's elder statesman, supported al-Afdal but the latter proved incompetent so al-Adil shifted his support to al-Aziz. Together they drove al-Afdal out of Damascus, but al-Aziz died in 1198 and the Egyptian army, which was the largest of the Ayyubid forces, split into two factions supporting either al-Adil or al-Afdal. Eventually al-Adil prevailed and was proclaimed Sultan over both Egypt and Syria while al-Afdal was sent into retirement at Samsat. He re-emerged in 1216 and tried to take over Aleppo, supported by the Saljuq Sultan of Konya. However, the Saljuqs were routed, and al-Afdal lost all his Syrian fiefs and returned to obscurity as a dependant of the Saljuq Sultan. He died at Samsat in AD 1225, but his body was brought to Aleppo for burial. Some say al-Afdal was interred next to his mother; others that it was near Shaykh al-Harawi the famous traveller and military adviser to Saladin.

Sarim al-Din Qaymaz al-Najmi was one of those senior but non-political officers who feature in the historical records for a few years, then disappear again. His honorific name Sarim al-Din or 'Cutting-edge of the Faith' shows him to have been a Muslim and may reflect his character. His personal name Qaymaz reveals him to have been a Turk, and his affiliation al-Najmi shows he was a slave-recruited soldier who had been purchased, trained, freed and employed by Saladin's father, Najm al-Din Ayyub.

Imad al-Din al-Isfahani described Sarim al-Din as, 'a valiant swordsman, a resolute chief, a skilled warrior, a lion charging at his target, the most daring and the most praiseworthy man, at the head of 500 cavalry endowed with vigour, courage and energy.' This figure of 500 troops was also mentioned on other occasions. In May 1187 Sarim al-Din was one of the 'two leading *amirs*' who went with Muzaffar al-Din Göbari, the ruler of Harran and Edessa, and Saladin's son al-Afdal to ravage the area of Saffuriya. There they routed a force of Hospitallers and killed the Grand Master. After this victory Saladin wrote a letter in which he praised 'our *mamluk* Sarim al-Din Qaymaz'.

At this time he was leader of the *mamluks* based in Damascus. Sarim al-Din was made governor of Tiberius after it was regained following the battle of Hattin and was described as a 'great dignitary'. The castle of

Figures representing court officials were also popular in the Saljuq-style art of northern Iraq, even appearing on this 12th- or 13th-century earthenware water-cooling pot from Mosul. (National Museum, Damascus; author's photograph)

The court life of early medieval Egypt was illustrated on the carved wooden doors of the Fatimid Caliphal Palace, which Saladin probably continued to use during the first years of his rule. (Museum of Islamic Art, Cairo; author's photograph)

Beaufort was offered to many other *amirs* before Saladin virtually forced it upon Sarim al-Din who was not interested in civilian administration, being a soldier at heart. Sarim al-Din Qaymaz played a significant role during the siege of Acre where he fought in the front ranks and was described by the chronicler Baha' al-Din as a *tawashi* or senior officer of the *tawashi mamluks*. He and his men tended to be placed on the right wing. Sarim al-Din was also sometimes given an independent command. He still seems to have been leader of the Damascus *mamluks*, perhaps of all the elite troops from Damascus, during the siege of Acre and he almost certainly led them at the battle of Arsuf where he again distinguished himself.

1 D. Carpenter, *The Struggle for Mastery, Britain 1066–1284*, London (2003), p.246.
2 M. Bennett, 'The Composition of Crusader Hosts, 1096–1192' (unpublished paper read at Reading University Extra-Mural Section, 9 March 1995).

OPPOSING FORCES

THE CRUSADER ARMIES

The recruitment of Crusaders was based upon extended households and dependency relationships within military aristocracies, urban elites and that part of the non-noble rural populations with disposable assets – in other words, those who could afford to go on Crusade. Only free men were allowed to 'take the cross', although some serfs or bondsmen were freed so that they could do so. A major exception to this rule were the enslaved *ministeriales* of Germany (see further description later in this chapter). Some condemned criminals also travelled as part of their punishment. Military contingents were organized around rulers, lords and knights. Beneath this elite came large numbers of servants who travelled with their masters, and people of rural or urban origin with useful skills. The motives of the overwhelming majority were religious, rather than financial or social. Crusading was, in fact, very expensive and many knights ruined themselves financially by going on crusade. The reliance on charity which had been a feature of some early crusades was no longer adequate, so, with the exception of the senior leadership, virtually every man and woman on the Third Crusade was paid in some way by somebody.

The defeat of previous crusades was blamed on pride, arrogance, overconfidence and love of luxury – not on the military and political capabilities of the Muslim foe. While God might punish the Christians for their sinfulness, God obviously could not support their enemies! So, before the Third Crusade was assembled, the Council of Le Mans drew up sumptuary laws which stated that none should wear 'vair, gris, sable or scarlet'. There would also be a theoretical ban on the presence of women other than laundry women of high reputation and close relatives of some of the Crusader leadership.

Since few participants had previous experience of Middle Eastern warfare, they took with them expectations and attitudes reflecting military action in 12th-century Europe. This was characterized by raiding, ravaging enemy territory and sieges, with very few major battles. Sieges rarely included the suicidal assaults upon towers and walls beloved of modern film-makers. Instead they were usually a matter of patience, endurance, starvation, disease, mutual bombardment, occasional raids or sorties, and an almost 20th-century form of close trench warfare.

Major economic developments within Europe enabled some rulers and great lords to become almost independent of feudal vassals upon whom they no longer depended for military support. King Richard of England had reached this enviable position, and the King of France would soon have enough money to conduct major campaigns without too much reliance on his great barons. As a result knights almost became

The primitive English wall paintings at Claverley illustrate the style of arms and armour used by English knights during the Third Crusade. (*In situ* Church of All Saints, Claverley; author's photograph)

The vulnerability of early crossbowmen is well illustrated in this 12th-century mosaic from northern Italy. The soldier's weapon is also of an early form with a wooden rather than composite bow. (*In situ* Church of San Colombano, Bobio; photograph Associazione culturale 'Amici di Archivum Bobiense')

employees of the king. The situation was even more revolutionary where professional infantry were concerned. These troops were vital in siege warfare and the easiest way to recruit them was simply to hire them.

The most renowned mercenaries in 12th-century Western Europe were the Brabançones, Flemings and Cottereaux, most of whom seem to have been spearmen rather than crossbowmen. All three groups were employed in England, Aquitaine and France. In open battle, however, such troops were only effective when cavalry protected their flanks. Archers and even crossbowmen still had low military status, despite often being highly skilled, and, given the social attitudes of the time, it is not surprising to see ordinary soldiers being treated little better than beasts of burden, even on the Third Crusade.

Although the crossbow had been known in parts of Europe for centuries, it first became widely popular in northern Italy in the 1140s. Crossbows incorporating very powerful bowstaves of composite construction begin to be mentioned in the late 12th century, but it is unclear how widespread they were at the battle of Arsuf. Modern research shows that the maximum pull for a crossbow with an iron stirrup when spanned with the simple hip-belt and hook used during this period, was 150kg. This would pack a considerable punch. The 'two feet crossbow', spanned by placing both feet on the bow, shot a more expensive and presumably heavier quarrel or arrow.

Most developments in European armour during this period were in response to the threat from crossbows and perhaps ordinary bows as well. They included not only helmets which covered more of the face and neck, but also the earliest references to semi-rigid body armour and a sudden revival in the use of horse armour – a very expensive form of protection which had virtually disappeared from Western Europe with the fall of the Roman Empire. There has been widespread misunderstanding about the strength of European armour, and the supposed weakness of Islamic archery, during the Third Crusade. What the written sources indicate is that Crusader armour was effective against long-range harassment archery using composite bows and relatively light arrows, but much less effective at close range. When Muslim archers came close, Crusader infantry countered with crossbows, whose slow rate of shooting was less of a problem than sometimes thought. Crossbowmen often shot in relays – load, prepare, shoot. Furthermore, horse archers on the move did not shoot with the astonishing rapidity that a fully trained Muslim archer could achieve when he or his horse was standing still. Shooting on the move involved mounted units approaching rapidly, shooting, perhaps only once, and then withdrawing equally rapidly before repeating this manoeuvre.

It would be misleading to call the army led by King Richard of England English or British, since a substantial part of it came from the Angevin provinces of France. Its ranks included a substantial part of the Angevin aristocracy from England and the western provinces of France, plus many members of the ecclesiastical elite. The military leaders were described as tried and tested 'men of renown', but they also included some, like Earl William I of Derby, whose families ranked low within England's aristocracy. In fact Earl William's death during the siege of Acre brought great prestige to his family, the Ferrers, who had not enjoyed much of a military reputation previously.[3]

Much less is known about men from lower down the social scale who took the cross in the late 1180s and early 1190s. The *Assize of Arms*, drawn up by King Henry II in 1181, still formed the basis of military recruitment in Angevin England, but payment of a tax called *scutage* as an alternative to personal military service, became general in the second half of the 12th century. This provided the king with money to hire professionals. Even so, the obligation of landowners above a certain wealth to provide a *balistarius* or crossbowman for military service was so common that a leading legal scholar known as Glanvill, writing between 1187 and 1189, used the associated document as an archetypal *writ of right* in his legal treatise.

The role of non-military personnel was of course also vital. Religious leaders and administrators were also needed. When King Richard went on crusade the Keeper of the King's Seal, Roger Malus Catulus, went with him but was drowned off Cyprus on 24 April 1191. The Great Seal was lost, though later recovered. There is no record of official hospitals during the Third Crusade, but we know that the sick or injured were normally taken to the nearest friendly town for treatment. The only doctors whose names are recorded were senior members of their profession who formed part of the retinues of the great. Gilbertus Anglicus may have travelled east in the service of the Bishop of Salisbury or of the Earl of Leicester. He later became the most famous English doctor of his time. At least one field hospital was established by English troops during the siege of

This carving shows a fully armoured knight, equipped in a typical late 12th-century German style. (Castle Museum, Wartburg; author's photograph)

The carvings of early 13th-century armoured knights on the facade of Wells Cathedral in England include a man wearing an early form of great helm.

A 12th-century carved ivory chess piece from southern France, wearing a style of segmented round helmet popular in these Mediterranean regions. (Museo del Bargello, Florence; author's photograph)

Acre, organized by a priest named William and dedicated to St Thomas à Becket.

A small amount of surviving evidence sheds a little light on how military equipment was assembled for a massive expedition like the Third Crusade. Most crossbows would have been imported by Genoese merchants, but within a year of Richard coming to the throne, the Pipe Roll accounts for the year 1189–90 refer to a payment to William Puintel, constable of the Tower of London, for the cost of making weapons there, including crossbows and crossbow bolts. Meanwhile the Sheriff of Gloucester provided 50,000 horseshoes for the Crusade.

Philip Augustus' army was recruited and organized along similar lines to that of King Richard. Compared to that of the Angevin realm, the political and financial administration of Capetian France was relatively backward, though based upon the same principles. After meeting Richard on the frontier with Normandy, both kings ordered a tax on all property and sources of revenue to pay for their forthcoming crusade. French Crusaders were also allowed two years' respite for the payment of existing debts and the tithe for the Holy War took precedence over all other financial obligations. Laymen were bound by an oath to pay the tithe, clergy by threat of excommunication. Landless knights paid the money to their lord or, if they had no lord, to the lord of the district in which they lived. Many individuals mortgaged their property in order to raise cash to join the Crusade, and many Crusaders had already given land to monasteries in return for money; the financing of crusades affected almost all aspects of life in 12th-century France.

Most information about the army of Philip Augustus dates from the first years of the 13th century, after he returned from the Third Crusade. By then the French king was richer and more powerful than he had been around 1190, but the main characteristics are unlikely to have differed (see Osprey Men-at-Arms 231: *French Medieval Armies 1000–1300*). The numbers involved in warfare within France during this period were small, though in theory much larger numbers were available. For example the *Feoda Campanie* was an ambitious effort by the Counts of Champagne to make a complete inventory of their feudal vassals. The first list, drawn up around 1172, was revised several times before 1192, and included the names of about 1,900 knights grouped into 26 *castellanies*. One copy in book form was actually taken to the Holy Land by Count Henry III in 1190 but was lost there. Nevertheless, the army which Philip Augustus brought to the siege of Acre was smaller than that of Richard, which surprised Muslim observers who regarded France as the most formidable crusading power in Western Europe.

The lords who formed the leadership of the French contingent included the Duke of Burgundy, the Counts of Flanders, Troyes, Blois, Sancerre, Dreux, Nevers, Clermont, Ponthieu and Perche, plus several senior churchmen. The only senior baron to remain at home was the Count of Toulouse. Furthermore, Count Philippe of Flanders, the Count of Blois and his brother the royal seneschal, Count Henry of Troyes and Count Etienne of Sancerre all died during this campaign.

Unlike King Richard and King Philip Augustus, the Emperor Frederick Barbarossa of Germany already had experience of crusading, having taken part in the Second Crusade's failed assault on Damascus. His position in Germany was also unusually strong in 1188 when virtually

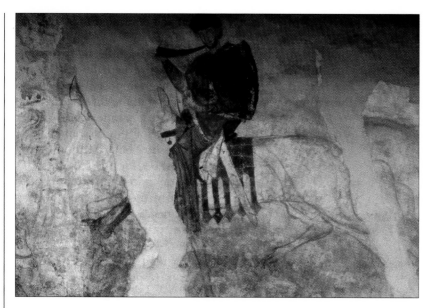

The paintings which once adorned the outside of many medieval churches survive in very few places. This rare example shows a knight with a helmet and shield riding in a typically decorated late 12th-century saddle. (*In situ* Castel Appiano; author's photograph)

Although military equipment was very similar throughout Western Europe in the late 12th and early 13th centuries, mail coifs indicated by the extensions of these soldiers' chests, may have been adopted earlier in Imperial territory than in France or England. (*In situ* Church of St. Trophime, Arles; author's photograph)

all the ruling princes of the Empire gathered at Mainz to discuss the forthcoming Third Crusade. Nevertheless, Emperor Frederick's was the least successful of the three main expeditions.

The main reason was, of course, the Emperor's death before reaching the Holy Land, but there were other significant weaknesses in the German contribution. Compared with the Angevin Empire and France, Imperial Germany was financially and militarily backward – despite being rich with a huge pool of military manpower. The funding of the German contingents also largely fell upon the Emperor himself. According to the English chronicler Raduphus Niger, Frederick Barbarossa did not ask his subjects to pay special taxes but financed the Crusade by imposing what later became known as a hearth tax, to which the Emperor's own family demesne and that of the public treasury also contributed.

German troops had often campaigned outside their own country and may have been more experienced than the French or English in this respect. One of the most important groups to be involved in such campaigns were the *ministeriales* who, though technically having a legal status comparable to that of serfs, were already a military elite. *Ministeriales* were normally expected to have a warhorse, a trotter or ordinary riding horse, and a packhorse on campaign. German knights in the army that Emperor Frederick Barbarossa took to Italy in 1161 were also instructed to have servants, mail hauberks, weapons, provisions, extra horseshoes and goatskin coats against the cold. *Ministeriales* on such expeditions were not expected to bear the full costs, and instead received grants from their lords; although it is unclear whether similar arrangements were made for the Third Crusade, it seems likely.

The German response to the preaching of the Third Crusade was certainly impressive, and in 1189 the Emperor Frederick Barbarossa was accompanied by his younger son Duke Frederick of Swabia, his former chancellor Geoffrey now the Bishop of Würzburg, ten other bishops and innumerable secular magnates including 28 counts; the list of participants fills five pages in the *Historia de expeditione Frederici imperatoris.*

Perhaps bearing in mind his previous experience of crusading, Frederick Barbarossa put considerable effort into ensuring strict discipline. Before his crusading army crossed the border into Hungary he issued a special Law of War which would apply to everyone. To quote R. Hiestand: 'The first to suffer under it were not humble crusaders, but nobles caught red-handed, stealing and robbing, who were put to death without pardon.'[4]

Most of the existing medieval fortifications of the bustling city of Damascus like the Bab al-Faradis date from the 13th century, though they were erected on the site of previous defences. (Author's photograph)

The army led by the German Emperor Frederick Barbarossa was one of the biggest and best equipped in the history of the Crusades. The 'Army of King Turnus' shown in this late 12th-century *Eneit* manuscript shows typical German knights of the period. (Preussische Staatsbibliothek, Ms. Germ. Fol. 282, Berlin)

Northern Italy was one of the most technologically advanced parts of Europe at the time of the Third Crusade, so its armies tended to be well equipped. (*In situ* Cathedral of San Donnino, Fidenza; author's photograph)

The massive 13th-century Hospitaller citadel in Acre was built upon the foundations of an earlier structure which formed part of the defences which defied the Third Crusade for two years. (Author's photograph)

The Italian contribution to the Third Crusade did not consist of a distinct Italian contingent led by an Italian ruler. In fact, Italy's main contribution was naval, without which this crusade could hardly have happened in the first place. Genoa and Pisa also provided troops, largely from the crews of their ships and including significant numbers of highly trained crossbowmen. These Italians also had the most advanced siege technology available to the Third Crusade, Lombardy being a major centre of advanced technology in the 12th century, while the Genoese reputation as siege engineers was clearly linked to their naval technology. Southern Italy and Sicily were different, and in military as well as some cultural matters they had as much in common with the Byzantine world and Islamic Egypt as they did with the rest of Italy. In the immediate aftermath of Saladin's virtual obliteration of the Kingdom of Jerusalem, a Norman–Sicilian fleet played a vital role supporting Tyre, but thereafter the region withdrew from the scene.

Having lost practically all its territory to Saladin, the Crusader Kingdom of Jerusalem was not in a position to contribute much to the Crusade which came to save it. Most of what remained of its military potential was already likely to have been committed to the siege of Acre, which began well before any large Crusader contingents arrived. Nevertheless, the army of the Kingdom of Jerusalem still existed to some extent, and the Arab chronicler Baha' al-Din saw the Kingdom's banner during the siege of Acre. It was, he wrote, 'on a staff as tall as a minaret, set up on a cart drawn by mules. It had a white ground with red spots, and the top of the staff was surmounted by a Cross.'[5]

The Military Orders already formed the military backbone of the Crusader States. So far, however, there were really only two Orders in the east: the Templars (see Osprey Warrior 91: *Knight Templar 1120–1312*) and the Hospitallers (see Osprey Warrior 33: *Knight Hospitaller [1] 1100–1306*). Their role, status and importance were evolving rapidly, the Hospitallers having been been militarized though they never lost their medical role. By the time of the Third Crusade each Order provided a regiment of a few hundred highly trained and motivated brother knights, plus some *turcopoles* and sergeants, though the latter had little military role in the late 12th century. Their tactics were within the Western European tradition and only their superior skill and discipline set them apart from other knightly cavalry.

Despite being resident experts in warfare against the Muslims, the Military Orders were generally more sympathetic to the aggressive attitudes of newly arrived Crusaders from Europe than to the more cautious military behaviour of resident Latins. On the other hand their leaders were aware of the Crusaders' limitations, as would become clear when the Grand Masters of both Military Orders urged King Richard to abandon his winter assault upon Jerusalem.

ISLAMIC FORCES

The late 12th century was an important period in the military history of the Islamic Middle East, being on the cusp of a gradual change from essentially Arab–Persian systems of recruitment, tactics and technology to a system strongly influenced by Turkish and subsequently also by Mongol military traditions. Saladin's armies clearly reflected a mixture of old and new ideas. At their centre was a corps of professional cavalry, trained and equipped not only in horse-archery but also for close combat. The elite included heavily armoured horsemen, sometimes on armoured horses who served as a commander's shock cavalry. Around this corps of professional cavalrymen were larger numbers of semi-professional cavalry and infantry, most of whom are best described as auxiliaries.

A particularly interesting aspect of Saladin's reign was his patronage of military writers and theoreticians. Three military texts survive which were either completed or were being composed during Saladin's reign. Al-Shayzari's work largely focused on military administration while al-Tarsusi's interests were technical and tactical, and al-Harawi wrote on theoretical, tactical, strategic and psychological aspects of warfare. Al-Harawi is the most interesting where the Third Crusade and the battle of Arsuf are concerned. The author was a scholar, served almost as one

One of the best illustrations of the type of heavily armoured cavalryman who formed the offensive elite of Saladin's army is on an early 13th-century bridge, which once spanned the river Tigris in the north-eastern corner of Syria. (*In situ* Ain Diwar; author's photograph)

of Saladin's secret agents and was present in Palestine during some of these events. The degree to which Saladin's strategy mirrors the ideas expounded by al-Harawi is remarkable.

The recruitment of Saladin's armies changed during his reign. He started with a very small army based in Egypt, having dispersed the bulk of the pre-existing Fatimid army because it was either overtly antagonistic or potentially unreliable. As a result the Nubian or sub-Saharan African element almost disappeared, along with the Armenian corps and the Berbers. Arab troops were similarly downgraded and as a result Saladin's armies were dominated by Turks and Kurds. Although there would be tension between Turks and Kurds under Saladin's Ayyubid successors, this was rare in Saladin's own time when both groups saw themseves as soldiers of Islam.

The most distinctive elite within Saladin's army were the slave-recruited *mamluks* or *ghulams*, mostly of pagan Central Asian Turkish origin, in a system of recruitment which went back to pre-Islamic times (see Osprey Men-at-Arms 259: *The Mamluks 1250–1517*). At the end of a recruit's education and training, he received a written certificate and was freed. The new soldier was also given a horse, clothing and military equipment before joining his regiment. These soldiers were usually known by the name of the ruler or senior military figure who 'recruited' them in the sense of buying the slaves and paying for their education and training. The bond of loyalty between the qualified *mamluk* and the commander who had previously also been his master was extremely strong, generally much stronger, in fact, than that between a Western European knight and his feudal lord.

Despite Saladin's clear mistrust of troops associated with the now defunct Fatimid Caliphate, they remained necessary to build an army big enough to defend his huge realm. As a result, *sudani* or 'black' African and even Masmuda Berbers from the western Sahara were recorded as late as AD 1191–92. Other old-style troops included Bedouin Arab tribal levies and former Fatimid soldiers now simply

RIGHT **A horseman wearing the fur-lined hat and double-breasted tunic of the Turkish military elite, on a late 12th- or early 13th-century ceramic plate from Iran. (Reza Abbasi Museum, Tehran; author's photograph)**

A foot soldier on the early 13th-century carved gate at Sinjar in north-western Iraq.

called 'Egyptians' who were recruited as mercenaries when required.

Some of Saladin's senior military leaders were freeborn while others were *mamluks*. For example Baha' al-Din Qaragush seems to have been a eunuch of Armenian origin. He was sent to refortify Acre and was captured when it fell to the Crusaders. As a very senior man, Qaragush was amongst the few who were spared when the garrison and inhabitants were massacred. Though a great builder of fortifications, bridges and palaces, he had enemies within Saladin's government. One was Ibn Mammati, the chief of Saladin's army *diwan* or War Office whose book, *The Foolishness of Qaragush's Decisions*, contributed to the fact that the unfortunate Armenian eunuch is now recalled across the Middle East as a figure of fun.

The forces available to Saladin included provincial contingents as well as the main army based in Egypt (see Osprey Men-at-Arms 171: *Saladin and the Saracens*; and Warrior 10: *Saracen Faris 1050–1250 AD*). These were structured along the same lines, with local rulers purchasing as many *mamluks* as they could afford. Nevertheless, their size reflected the wealth of the province in question. Under Saladin's immediate successors the regional Ayyubid armies have been estimated as 4,000 in the Jazira, 2,000 in Mosul, 1,000 in Aleppo, 1,000 troops in Damascus, 1,000 in Hamah, Shayzar and other nearby castles, but only 500 in Hims. They also varied in composition as different ethnic groups and traditions were available in different regions.

For example, the Kurdish Hakkari tribe would become particularly important in the army of Aleppo. However, Turkoman and Kurdish tribal forces were notably hard to control, and where such troops played a dominant role, the long-term reliability, if not the skill or enthusiasm, of a provincial army could be questionable.

Some of the major cities of northern Iraq, the Jazira and Syria also differed from those of Egypt in still having urban militias who provided large numbers of infantry who were often skilled in siege warfare. While most *mamluks* were of Turkish origin, the tribal Turkomans were a separate military group. Their tribes roamed the northern regions of Saladin's empire. Some aristocratic families of Turkoman origin also controlled castles or even towns and, as Saladin's vassals, were expected to supply military contingents.

Infantry formed a vital but too often neglected part of Saladin's army. They were essential in siege warfare and played a prominent – if not very

The largely Kurdish provinces of south-eastern Turkey provided Saladin's armies with many of their soldiers. However, Hasankayf overlooking the river Tigris was not conquered by Saladin's Ayyubid successors until 1232. (Author's photograph)

A tall, flat-bottomed infantry shield is illustrated in this fine lustreware bowl, which was probably made in Egypt in the late 12th or very early 13th century. (Keir Collection, London)

successful – role in the battle of Arsuf. There is no evidence that these *rajjala* were organized into recognizable units but they appear in the chronicles as more than an amorphous horde of foot soldiers. They defended and assaulted fortifications and entrenchments in an organized manner, as well as operating siege machines which presupposed a considerable degree of command and control. Accounts of the battle of

This illustration of the Betrayal of Christ comes from a Coptic Gospel made in Damietta in AD 1179–80. The soldiers on the right probably reflect the low status of infantry who formed a major part of Saladin's army. (Bib. Nat., Ms. Copte 13, f.79r, Paris)

The bulk of Saladin's army consisted of Turks, like the long-haired men in fur hats in the rear of this picture, or Kurds. The main role of Arab-speakers was in the administration or medical support services. (*Kitab al-Tiryaq*, Ms. Arabe 2964, f. 17, Bib. Nat., Paris)

Arsuf itself make it clear that the large numbers of infantrymen advanced in clearly distinguishable groups ahead of, and in co-ordination with, equally defined mounted units. Statements in military treatises like that of al-Harawi, which assume infantry to have been as structured and controlled as cavalry units, have often been dismissed as reflecting an ancient ideal which no longer existed by Saladin's time. Closer reading of contemporary chronicles, however, offers a different picture; one in which infantry fought in a remarkably organized manner.

Their ranks consisted of trained mercenaries, religiously motivated volunteers – some with and many without military skills – assorted 'rabbles' who were not necessarily as chaotic as their name suggests, and Arab Bedouin tribal auxiliaries. The *harafish*, whose name actually means 'rabble', were even mentioned as military specialists, fighting like modern-day commandos inside enemy territory. On other occasions the *harafishah* are described as beggars, living on handouts from powerful men, who formed militias or armed gangs in times of political trouble.

These assorted volunteers formed a low-status military reserve, difficult to control but useful nonetheless. The large numbers of foot soldiers whom Saladin summoned to his counter-siege of the Crusader army besieging Acre included large numbers of *aswad* (black) and other troops who arrived from Egypt under al-Adil. Meanwhile Saladin recruited infantry under his own immediate command from Syria. Unfortunately neither Arab nor European accounts of the Third Crusade are very clear on the identity of soldiers involved. The name Nubians comes up occasionally, and the Christian kingdoms of Nubia in what is now northern Sudan were still militarily potent during this period. Nubians were famous as infantry archers and, like so many medieval peoples along the southern fringes of the Sahara desert, they fought with large powerful bows of simple rather than composite construction. On the other hand, Nubian soldiers were also described in this period as having 'no defence' against the arrows of Saladin's and his successors' Turkish troops. Some evidence also hints at the possibility that significant sections of the ex-Fatimid military system survived in southern Egypt and along the Red Sea coast. In both these regions Saladin also tried to maintain reasonable relations with the Arab Bedouin tribes who had previously been loyal supporters of the Fatimids.

Arab auxiliaries were normally kept apart from the Turkoman and Kurdish troops. The tribes from which they were drawn varied greatly in wealth and military potential but, in most cases, Arab Bedouin fought as infantry archers with small cavalry elites. The traditional Arab bow, unlike the Turkish bow, was a large weapon designed for use on foot and was made of wood rather than composite construction. Most of Saladin's Bedouin auxiliaries were recruited in the southern parts of the Fertile Crescent, Palestine, Sinai, the Eastern or Red Sea Desert, the Western or Libyan Desert and within the Nile Delta and the Nile Valley. Here many peasant communities retained a distinct and proudly Arab identity, separate from the communities descended from Coptic or pre-Islamic Egyptians. Such Arab troops often served in specialist roles as raiders and ambush troops, attacking enemy communications, largely because they had a reputation for speed and endurance. Rather more unexpectedly, some of the Bedouin of the eastern Nile Delta were troublesome river pirates, but whether Saladin was able to turn such skills to his naval advantage is unknown.

3 For a detailed account of the role of this particular aristocratic family in the Crusades, see: M.R. Evans, 'The Ferrers Earls of Derby and the Crusades' in *Nottingham Medieval Studies*, XLIV, (2000), pp.69–81.
4 R. Hiestand, 'Kingship and Crusade in C 12th Germany,' in A. Haverkamp (ed.), *England and Germany in the High Middle Ages*, Oxford (1996), pp.256–7.
5 Baha' al-Din Ibn Shaddad (tr. C.W. Wilson), *Saladin, what befell Sultan Yusuf*, Palestine Pilgrims' Text Society, London (1897), pp.226–7.

OPPOSING PLANS

KING RICHARD'S PLAN

King Richard's strategy was not to seek Saladin's army in a major battle. Instead, the Angevin king adopted the same cautious approach seen in his French campaigns. Such caution was far from unusual and Richard's strategic priorities were the same as those of most of his Western European contemporaries. Furthermore, winning a battle did not necessarily mean winning a war, and indeed Richard's successes at Arsuf and elsewhere did not bring victory for the Third Crusade. The main aim of European warfare during this period was to resort to battle only when all else had failed. Instead, most 12th-century western armies sought to take and hold territory through the capture of castles and fortified towns.

Having retaken Acre in the face of a powerful enemy field force, the Crusader army, now under the single command of King Richard, moved south to secure the coast. Without this, there was no chance of retaking Jerusalem. In the event their march from Acre to Jaffa has been interpreted as a classic example of the 'fighting march', with the battle of Arsuf merely being its most dramatic episode. Terrain was a major factor in such fighting marches and in Palestine the army of the Kingdom of Jerusalem had earlier shown reluctance to enter 'rocky terrain' disadvantageous to western-style armoured cavalry and their primary tactic of the charge. Indeed, Saladin was unfortunate in being obliged to launch his attack, just north of Arsuf, in terrain which was at least adequate from the point of view of Crusader cavalry.

In recent years there has been much discussion about the 'fighting march', especially with reference to the Third Crusade. Most of the debate focuses on how much Crusader commanders learned from Byzantine and Islamic military experience, and how much was a natural reaction to tactical conditions in the Middle East. Matthew Bennett has noted the Byzantine military ideal of a hollow formation with cavalry inside a protective box of infantry when marching through hostile territory in the face of an enemy strong in cavalry – precisely the formation adopted by King Richard during his march south from Acre. However, the same tactical philosophy was recommended by Arab and Persian military writers from the 9th to the 13th centuries. What cannot be disputed is King Richard's skill in using these perhaps well established tactics, and the leadership skills which enabled him to impose a close order of march upon his disparate army.

The tactic of the fighting march depended upon effective co-operation between cavalry and infantry. Here King Richard was fortunate in having at his disposal the elite forces of the Military Orders which had often provided vanguards and rearguards for Crusader armies on the march.

This tactic also needed reasonably disciplined foot soldiers whose role was to provide a human fortress from which the cavalry could launch charges and into which the cavalry could then withdraw. Normally such infantry tactics also included archers and crossbowmen whose task was to keep enemy troops at a distance.

SALADIN'S PLAN

Saladin's strategy was to contain and then expel the invaders. Having failed to save Acre, he knew that the Crusaders would try to take Jerusalem and to do this they would have to secure Jaffa as a naval supply base. The Crusader army's march down the coast from Acre to Jaffa was a necessary move which exposed them to attack and harassment by Saladin's army.

The battle of Arsuf has been described as a strong attack on an army on the march, rather than a confrontation in battle array.[6] However, this interpretation fails to appreciate the tactical traditions of the medieval Islamic World which were generally more mobile and faster moving than those of Western Europe. While surviving military manuals lay great emphasis on organizing a line of march, preparing the route and arraying an army so that its vulnerability was minimized, such manuals give equal importance to the ambushing of these columns.

Where battles or even major skirmishes were concerned, the military tradition in which Saladin operated put primary emphasis on co-ordination between cavalry and infantry. The most important of the latter were archers, both infantry and mounted, whose role was not only static and defensive but also mobile and offensive. Horsemen operated from the protection of men on foot, above all infantry archers and, where cavalry were concerned, the primary emphasis was still on close combat with spears rather than upon horse-archers.[7] The similarities between this sort of warfare, as described in theoretical sources, and the battle of Arsuf as recorded by contemporary chroniclers is remarkable.

Earlier medieval Islamic chroniclers occasionally mentioned successful attacks being made when an enemy army was coming to the end of a day's march, at the moment called *nuzul* when enemy soldiers were tired, thirsty, and eager to claim a good place for their tent. The enemy commander's authority might be weakened at that point, and his men's determination, as well as their cohesion, might also be fractured. The *nuzul* was not, of course, necessarily at the close of the day, but merely at the end of the day's march. Surely Saladin's decision to attack when and where he did on the day of the battle of Arsuf was fully within this tactical tradition.

Absolutely central to Islamic tactics during this and earlier centuries was the effort to separate enemy cavalry from their infantry. Saladin had done this on previous occasions against both Muslim and Crusader foes. He tried it again at Arsuf, initially with some success though in the end he failed. Al-Harawi, whose book of military advice for Saladin or his immediate successor has already been mentioned, offered other advice which is mirrored in the battle of Arsuf. This included sending infantry into the attack ahead of cavalry; and these foot soldiers should include archers shooting both 'ordinary' and heavy arrows, in addition to javelin throwers with light and heavy javelins. Accounts of the battle of Arsuf hint that

Saladin followed another bit of al-Harawi's advice, drawing up his troops to match the foe's array, best for best and type for type, though this is less clear. When the enemy attacked or counterattacked, the commander should send some of his cavalry and infantry against that section of the enemy line from which the attack had been launched, because it would now be weaker. There is no evidence that Saladin was able to do this at Arsuf, though his men did launch at least two counterattacks.[8]

6 J. Gillingham, 'Richard I and the science of war in the middle ages,' in J. Gillingham & J.C. Holt (eds.), *War and Government in the Middle Ages: Essays in Honour of J.O. Prestwich*, Woodbridge (1984), p.80.

7 See the Fatimid abbreviation of a classical 'Abbasid military text by Abu Sa'id al-Sha'rani al-Harthami (ed. 'Abd al-Rawf 'Awn & Muhammad Mustafa Ziyadah) Mukhtasar Siyasat al-Hurub, Cairo (1964), passim.

8 Al-Harawi (ed. & trans. J. Sourdel-Thomine), 'Les Conseils du Sayh al Harawi à un Prince Ayyubide' in Bulletin d'Etudes Orientales de l'Institut Francais de Damas, XVII, (1961–62), pp.233–4; note that the French translation is incorrect where the weapons of the attacking infantry are concerned.

THE CAMPAIGN

EVENTS GATHER PACE

Although the Third Crusade started with the preaching of a crusade to regain Jerusalem in 1188, events were already unfolding in the Middle East. In fact, the struggle had not ceased with Saladin's military successes the previous year (see Osprey Campaign 19: *Hattin 1187*). Rather, resistance to Saladin's seemingly inexorable advance increased when Conrad of Monferrat arrived in Tyre on 14 July 1187 and convinced those defending the city to break off surrender negotiations. Saladin meanwhile had other things to consider, including exchanging diplomatic gifts with the Emperor Isaac II Angelus as part of his broader effort to cement good relations with the Byzantine Empire. On the other hand, Saladin's relations with his religious suzerain, the 'Abbasid Caliph in Baghdad, remained difficult. On 9 February 1188 there was a fatal brawl between military forces guarding the Muslim *Haj* pilgrim caravan from Damascus (largely from Saladin's domain) and those protecting the *Haj* caravan from Iraq (largely from the Caliph's own domain).

Saladin's primary military concern during 1188 was, of course, to mop up or contain what remained of the Crusader States. In March he inspected the siege of Belvoir, then returned to Damascus to assemble additional troops. On 14 May Saladin's army marched north but found Tripoli too strong to be besieged, so Saladin took as many Crusader fortifications as he could in north-western Syria, concluding with the capture of Baghras and the signing of a truce with the now paralysed Principality of Antioch. After demobilizing his northern vassal contingents Saladin returned to Damascus; his own troops continuing to blockade Safad and Belvoir throughout the winter of 1188–89.

Another panel from the carved wooden doors of the Caliph's Palace in Cairo is decorated with a scene of a caravan, a camel with a howdah and two caravan guards. (Museum of Islamic Art, Cairo; author's photograph)

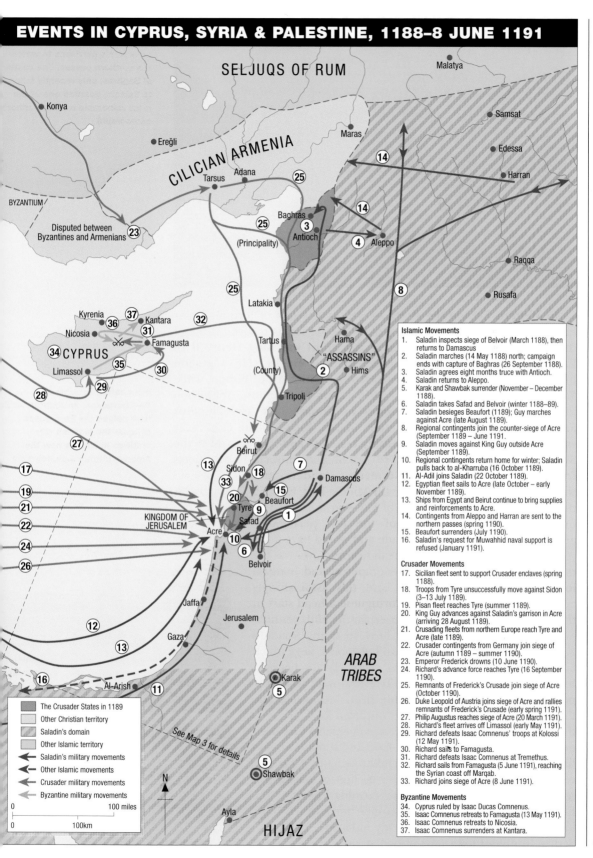

SELJUQS OF RUM

Malatya

Konya

Samsat

Ereğli

Edessa

Maras

CILICIAN ARMENIA

Tarsus   Adana

Harran

BYZANTIUM

(25)

Disputed between
Byzantines and Armenians (23)

(14)

(25)

Baghras

(14)

Antioch (3)

Aleppo (4)

(Principality)

Raqqa

(25)

Latakia

(8)

Rusafa

Kyrenia (37)

Nicosia (36) Kantara (31)

(32)

Famagusta

Tartus

Hama

(34) CYPRUS

"ASSASSINS"

Limassol (35)

(30)

(County)

Hims (2)

(29)

(28)

Tripoli

(27)

Beirut

(17)

(13) Sidon

(18)

(7)

Damascus

(19)

(33)

(15)

(21)

(20) Beaufort

(22)

Tyre (9)

(1)

KINGDOM OF
JERUSALEM

Acre Safad

(24)

(10)

(26)

(6)

Belvoir

Jaffa

(12)

Jerusalem

(13)

Gaza

ARAB
TRIBES

(16)

Al-Arish (11)

Karak (5)

See Map 3 for details

(5) Shawbak

N

Ayla

HIJAZ

Legend

- ▨ The Crusader States in 1189
- ☐ Other Christian territory
- ▨ Saladin's domain
- ☐ Other Islamic territory
- ← Saladin's military movements
- ← Other Islamic movements
- ← Crusader military movements
- ← Byzantine military movements

0 ——————— 100 miles
0 ——————— 100km

Islamic Movements

1. Saladin inspects siege of Belvoir (March 1188), then returns to Damascus
2. Saladin marches (14 May 1188) north; campaign ends with capture of Baghras (26 September 1188).
3. Saladin agrees eight months truce with Antioch.
4. Saladin returns to Aleppo.
5. Karak and Shawbak surrender (November – December 1188).
6. Saladin takes Safad and Belvoir (winter 1188–89).
7. Saladin besieges Beaufort (1189); Guy marches against Acre (late August 1189).
8. Regional contingents join the counter-siege of Acre (September 1189 – June 1191).
9. Saladin moves against King Guy outside Acre (September 1189).
10. Regional contingents return home for winter; Saladin pulls back to al-Kharruba (16 October 1189).
11. Al-Adil joins Saladin (22 October 1189).
12. Egyptian fleet sails to Acre (late October – early November 1189).
13. Ships from Egypt and Beirut continue to bring supplies and reinforcements to Acre.
14. Contingents from Aleppo and Harran are sent to the northern passes (spring 1190).
15. Beaufort surrenders (July 1190).
16. Saladin's request for Muwahhid naval support is refused (January 1191).

Crusader Movements

17. Sicilian fleet sent to support Crusader enclaves (spring 1188).
18. Troops from Tyre unsuccessfully move against Sidon (3–13 July 1189).
19. Pisan fleet reaches Tyre (summer 1189).
20. King Guy advances against Saladin's garrison in Acre (arriving 28 August 1189).
21. Crusading fleets from northern Europe reach Tyre and Acre (late 1189).
22. Crusader contingents from Germany join siege of Acre (autumn 1189 – summer 1190).
23. Emperor Frederick drowns (10 June 1190).
24. Richard's advance force reaches Tyre (16 September 1190).
25. Remnants of Frederick's Crusade join siege of Acre (October 1190).
26. Duke Leopold of Austria joins siege of Acre and rallies remnants of Frederick's Crusade (early spring 1191).
27. Philip Augustus reaches siege of Acre (20 March 1191).
28. Richard's fleet arrives off Limassol (early May 1191).
29. Richard defeats Isaac Comnenus' troops at Kolossi (12 May 1191).
30. Richard sails to Famagusta.
31. Richard defeats Isaac Comnenus at Tremethus.
32. Richard sails from Famagusta (5 June 1191), reaching the Syrian coast off Marqab.
33. Richard joins siege of Acre (8 June 1191).

Byzantine Movements

34. Cyprus ruled by Isaac Ducas Comnenus.
35. Isaac Comnenus retreats to Famagusta (13 May 1191).
36. Isaac Comnenus retreats to Nicosia.
37. Isaac Comnenus surrenders at Kantara.

As the Emperor Frederick's army marched across Turkey, Saladin ordered his garrisons to watch the northern passes. The castle of Baghras, only recently fallen to Saladin, guarded one of the most vulnerable routes. (Author's photograph)

In Western Europe the shock caused by the loss of Jerusalem was rapidly followed by the preaching of a Crusade for its recovery. One of the most enthusiastic supporters of this effort was King Henry II of England, ruler of the huge Angevin feudal empire. He was soon followed by his son and soon to be successor, Richard of Poitou, while King Philip Augustus was more considered in his response. Yet he too joined Henry II in taking the cross in January 1188 and Emperor Frederick Barbarossa did the same in March. King William II of Sicily was amongst the first to do something concrete and in spring 1188 the Sicilian fleet sailed to support Tyre, Tripoli and Antioch. In May fleets from Denmark, northern Germany, Flanders and southern England also set sail for the Middle East; helping the Portuguese capture the city of Silves from the Moors on the way. This was one of the few permanent achievements of the Third Crusade and would have an as yet unexpected impact on European history. Silves was the main centre of Arab–Islamic geographical and nautical lore concerning the Atlantic, and this astonishingly advanced knowledge gave the Portuguese a head start in the great European Age of Discovery in the 15th century.

Events gathered pace during 1189. In spring Saladin's army besieged Beaufort in southern Lebanon, a siege which lasted until July 1190, and there were clashes between Saladin's troops and those from Tyre who were soon supported by a powerful Pisan battle fleet. Meanwhile, the Emperor Frederick Barbarossa set out from Regensburg at the head of a huge army in May. Arrangements had been made the previous year, whereby food and supplies should have been available to Frederick's host which was the largest contingent in the Third Crusade. Its line of march was sometimes three days long. After crossing Hungary, the Emperor entered nominally Byzantine territory in June, into what was in reality the already independent state of Serbia. In August his army stopped at Nish where Serbian

Even before entering the Mediterranean, an Anglo-Angevin fleet helped the Portuguese conquer the Moorish city of Silves in what is now the Algarve. (Author's photograph)

The Byzantine Emperor was so worried by the approach of the Emperor Frederick's huge crusading army that he insisted it cross into Anatolia via the Dardanelles, seen here, rather than coming any nearer to Constantinople (Istanbul). (Author's photograph)

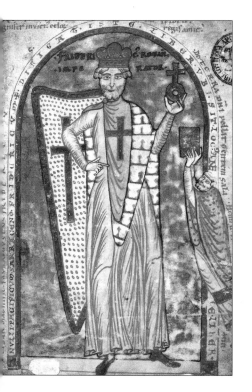

The Emperor Frederick of Germany shown as a Crusader in a manuscript made in AD 1188–89. (Bib. Apost., Ms. Lat. 2001, f.1r, Rome)

representatives, and some of those Bulgarians who were already in revolt against the Byzantine Empire, offered to form an anti-Byzantine alliance with Frederick. Although the German Emperor did not accept, his army went on to occupy the main Bulgarian city of Plovdiv, defeating a half-hearted Byzantine attempt to resist.

When Isaac Angelus sent two senior ambassadors to meet the Emperor Frederick, they turned against their own Emperor and encouraged Frederick to attack him! Isaac next seized Frederick's representatives as hostages, but Frederick countered by seeking papal approval for an anti-Byzantine Crusade and sent his son Henry to occupy Didymotikon. Relations between the two Emperors and their followers went from bad to worse while the German Crusaders settled in Edirne for the winter.

Eventually Isaac agreed to ferry the massive German Crusader army across the Dardanelles into Anatolia which would avoid the necessity of Frederick's troops passing through Constantinople. This they did in March 1190. There were minor clashes with local Byzantine troops before the Crusader army finally crossed the frontier into the Saljuq Sultanate of Rum. Some years earlier Frederick had tried to form an anti-Byzantine alliance with the Sultan of Rum, but that was now forgotten and on 17 May 1190 a Saljuq army under Sultan Kilij Arslan II's son Qutb al-Din attempted to stop the Germans entering the Saljuq capital of Konya. It was defeated but, although Konya fell, Frederick's army marched steadily onwards.

By the time they reached the Taurus mountains the Germans were running short of food and supplies for men and horses. As the Arab chronicler put it, they were 'forced to abandon a great quantity of baggage, and a number of armours, helmets and weapons, for want of transport.' Further on the Germans marched 'almost all without armour or spears', supposedly having had to burn the latter for fuel.[9] When the Crusaders finally emerged

TOP **Tradition maintains that the Emperor Frederick Barbarossa died while swimming in the Göksu at this point, where the river emerges from the Taurus mountains. (Author's photograph)**

LEFT **The Seljuq ruler of central Turkey tried to stop Frederick's army entering his capital of Konya, but his army was swept aside. This carving is of two mailed foot soldiers dated a few years later. (Museum of Turkish Art, Konya)**

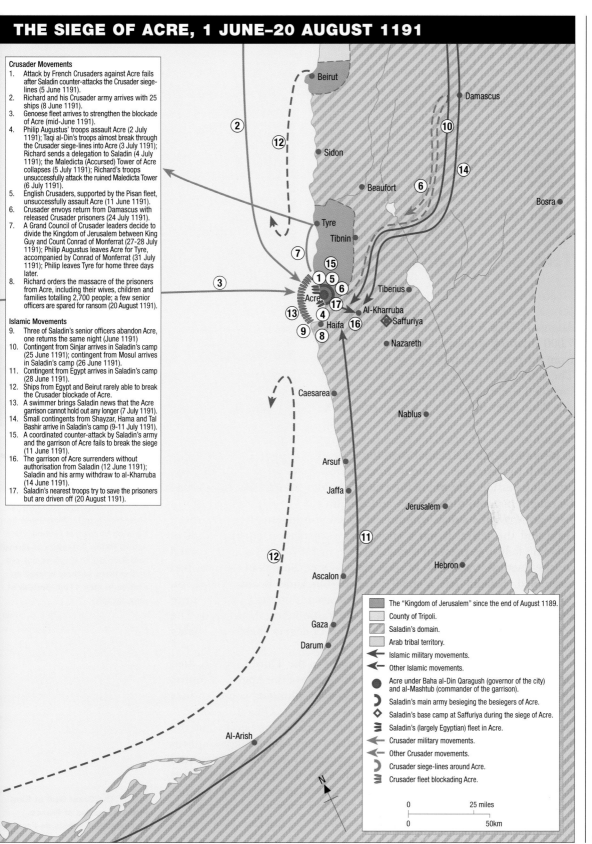

Crusader Movements

1. Attack by French Crusaders against Acre fails after Saladin counter-attacks the Crusader siege-lines (5 June 1191).
2. Richard and his Crusader army arrives with 25 ships (8 June 1191).
3. Genoese fleet arrives to strengthen the blockade of Acre (mid-June 1191).
4. Philip Augustus' troops assault Acre (2 July 1191); Taqi al-Din's troops almost break through the Crusader siege-lines into Acre (3 July 1191); Richard sends a delegation to Saladin (4 July 1191); the Maledicta (Accursed) Tower of Acre collapses (5 July 1191); Richard's troops unsuccessfully attack the ruined Maledicta Tower (6 July 1191).
5. English Crusaders, supported by the Pisan fleet, unsuccessfully assault Acre (11 June 1191).
6. Crusader envoys return from Damascus with released Crusader prisoners (24 July 1191).
7. A Grand Council of Crusader leaders decide to divide the Kingdom of Jerusalem between King Guy and Count Conrad of Monferrat (27-28 July 1191); Philip Augustus leaves Acre for Tyre, accompanied by Conrad of Monferrat (31 July 1191); Philip leaves Tyre for home three days later.
8. Richard orders the massacre of the prisoners from Acre, including their wives, children and families totalling 2,700 people; a few senior officers are spared for ransom (20 August 1191).

Islamic Movements

9. Three of Saladin's senior officers abandon Acre, one returns the same night (June 1191)
10. Contingent from Sinjar arrives in Saladin's camp (25 June 1191); contingent from Mosul arrives in Saladin's camp (26 June 1191).
11. Contingent from Egypt arrives in Saladin's camp (28 June 1191).
12. Ships from Egypt and Beirut rarely able to break the Crusader blockade of Acre.
13. A swimmer brings Saladin news that the Acre garrison cannot hold out any longer (7 July 1191).
14. Small contingents from Shayzar, Hama and Tal Bashir arrive in Saladin's camp (9-11 July 1191).
15. A coordinated counter-attack by Saladin's army and the garrison of Acre fails to break the siege (11 June 1191).
16. The garrison of Acre surrenders without authorisation from Saladin (12 June 1191); Saladin and his army withdraw to al-Kharruba (14 June 1191).
17. Saladin's nearest troops try to save the prisoners but are driven off (20 August 1191).

The "Kingdom of Jerusalem" since the end of August 1189.
County of Tripoli.
Saladin's domain.
Arab tribal territory.
Islamic military movements.
Other Islamic movements.
Acre under Baha al-Din Qaragush (governor of the city) and al-Mashtub (commander of the garrison).
Saladin's main army besieging the besiegers of Acre.
Saladin's base camp at Saffuriya during the siege of Acre.
Saladin's (largely Egyptian) fleet in Acre.
Crusader military movements.
Other Crusader movements.
Crusader siege-lines around Acre.
Crusader fleet blockading Acre.

0   25 miles

0   50km

N

from the Taurus Mountains and were approaching the Mediterranean where they could hope to have been resupplied by friendly fleets, disaster struck. The aged Emperor Frederick was drowned on 10 June, perhaps after suffering a heart attack, while swimming in the cold Göksu River and the huge but now demoralized German Crusader army fell apart. Meanwhile smaller German Crusader contingents from Cologne, Frisia, Bremen and Thuringia took the sea route from Venice to Palestine; the first travelling in autumn 1189, the last in summer 1190.

THE SIEGE OF ACRE

Meanwhile, King Guy, the nominal ruler of Jerusalem, had taken a bold initiative in August 1189 by leading about 400 knights and 7,000 infantry, supported by the Pisan fleet, from the relative safety of Tyre to besiege Acre. The latter had a garrison which, though small, included some of Saladin's elite troops, while the Pisan fleet was not yet strong enough to stop Saladin's ships from resupplying the city. Saladin considered attacking King Guy's army as it moved along the coastal road but instead decided to assemble a larger force before attacking outside Acre where the enemy could be caught between the garrison and Saladin's

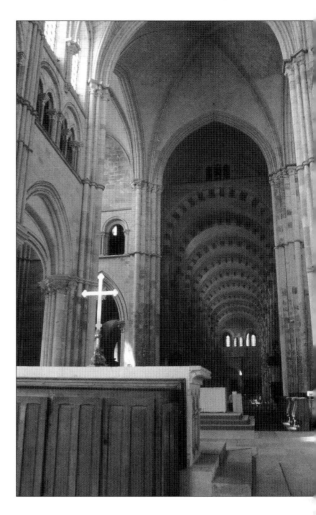

The church of La Madelaine at Vézelay in central France, from where Philip Augustus of France and Richard of England set out at the head of their crusading armies in July 1190. (Author's photograph)

field army. So the sultan summoned vassal contingents from northern Syria and the Jazira. It was a strategic miscalculation equal to that of Saladin's failure to press his assault on Tyre in 1187, but was again rooted in the tactical traditions of the time. Once sufficient troops had assembled, Saladin left a small force to blockade Beaufort and, on 15 September, moved against Guy. His first assault on the Crusader siege lines failed, just as King Guy's first assaults upon Acre had failed. The scene was set for a double siege, with the besiegers themselves being besieged, which would last until summer 1191.

King Henry II of England, a prime mover in the Third Crusade, died on 6 July 1189, and his son Richard became ruler of the Angevin Empire. In November King William II of Sicily also died, plunging southern Italy and Sicily into political confusion. His successor Queen Constance proved unacceptable and was replaced by Tancred of Lecce, but the Kingdom was still tense when King Richard and King Philip Augustus arrived the following year. These two kings actually left Vézelay in central France at the heads of their armies in July 1190, though the contingents took different routes by land and sea to Messina in Sicily. That summer Henry of Champagne led another French force directly to the siege of Acre while an Angevin advance force under Archbishop Baldwin of Canterbury also sailed directly to the Holy Land. While wintering in

RIGHT **The Great Seal of King Philip Augustus of France. (Archives Nationales de France, Paris)**

After Richard's troops landed in Messina in Sicily they found a country very different to their own. For example, the 12th-century Church of the Annunziata is a mixture of Byzantine and Arab styles. (Author's photograph)

Messina, relations between King Richard, King Philip Augustus and King Tancred of Sicily worsened, with serious clashes between the Crusaders and the local inhabitants, most of whom were Orthodox Christian Greeks in this part of Sicily.

After the death of Emperor Frederick Barbarossa, Duke Frederick of Swabia took command of the German Crusade while Saladin, not yet knowing that the Germans were in such a desperate state, ordered contingents from Harran and Aleppo to guard the northern passes. In fact, the remnants of Frederick's Crusade made their way by land and sea to the siege of Acre where Frederick of Swabia also died in January 1191. Another German Crusader contingent, this time led by Duke Leopold of Austria, had set out by sea from Venice and, after wintering at Zara in Croatia, reached the siege of Acre in spring 1191. Leopold now placed himself at the head of the remaining imperial troops.

Meanwhile the double siege of Acre continued. Neither side made any progress though both received reinforcements. On the other hand Saladin's naval squadrons, operating from Egypt and Lebanon, could not match the gradually increasing strength of Christian fleets. Once Philip Augustus and Richard arrived, the bulk of Saladin's navy was bottled up in Acre. Saladin's efforts to obtain naval help from the Muwahhid Caliph in Morocco were rebuffed, and instead the Muwahhids allowed Genoese ships to resupply in North African harbours on their way east.

The fighting around Acre now grew more intense, with Saladin's troops briefly breaking through the siege lines on 13 February 1191,

ANGLO-FRENCH FOLLOWERS OF KING RICHARD COEUR DE LION TEAR DOWN THE BANNER OF DUKE LEOPOLD OF AUSTRIA AND THROW IT INTO THE MOAT OF ACRE.
(pages 48–49)

King Richard managed to quarrel with almost all the other senior leaders of the Third Crusade, and a good number of the secondary commanders as well. Following the death of the Emperor Frederick Barbarossa the German imperial army disintegrated. Duke Leopold of Austria took command of its remnants, but these demoralized troops (1) were unable to play a significant role in the rest of the Crusade. On the other hand Leopold, as representative of the Empire and of what many people in Europe regarded as the most prestigious secular ruler in Christendom, insisted on having his banner (2) placed at an equal level to that of Richard of England (3) on the wall of Acre after the city had been conquered. In this reconstruction of the scene, the banner of King Philip Augustus is also shown (4). The French king was a diplomat before he was a warrior, and seems to have accepted Duke Leopold's banner as being politically if not militarily justified. King Richard's men (5), whether directly encouraged by him or not, felt otherwise and tore down Leopold's flag. They added insult to injury by throwing it into the moat. It was a humiliation which the Austrian ruler would not forget, and he thereafter remained a bitter enemy of King Richard of England. (Christa Hook)

This Italian carving of the Massacre of the Innocents is unusual in showing soldiers wearing quilted soft armour of a sort which was normally underneath a mail hauberk. It was made around AD 1200. (In situ Baptistry, Verona; Ian Peirce photograph)

bringing a relief army and a new commander into Acre. But for the defenders this was a temporary respite and Saladin was having difficulty keeping his army together. Even Taqi al-Din, Saladin's nephew and one of his most effective commanders, failed to rejoin the siege in the spring; instead being diverted by his own territorial ambitions in what is now south-eastern Turkey. He did eventually bring his troops to Acre, but Taqi al-Din's diversion was a sign of problems ahead for Saladin.

Whereas King Philip of France sailed directly from Sicily to the siege of Acre as soon as spring re-opened the sea routes, King Richard of England sailed via Crete and Rhodes, meeting storms on the way. He then turned aside to conquer the Byzantine island of Cyprus, ousting its rebel ruler Isaac Comnenus. Whether this was a brilliant piece of strategic thinking which provided future Crusades with a safe base in the Middle East, or was an unplanned reaction to Isaac Comnenus' treatment of Richard's shipwrecked followers remains a matter of debate. The diversion lasted the month of May, but would have a profound impact on the subsequent history of the eastern Mediterranean.

In the meantime French Crusaders under Philip Augustus threw their weight into the siege of Acre, eventually being joined by King Richard's 25 ships and larger army on 8 June. Richard's largely Anglo-French force was the last major contingent to arrive, except for a Genoese fleet whose appearance tipped the naval scales firmly in favour of the Crusaders. The siege remained long and bitter, with the Crusaders bombarding and assaulting the walls while Saladin's army tried to break through and relieve the garrison. Eventually, however, the troops within Acre could endure no more, and on 12 July 1191 they surrendered.

Acre capitulated without Saladin's authority, and by the time a swimmer from the city brought him the news it was too late for him to refuse. The terms of surrender involved all the ships in harbour being handed over,

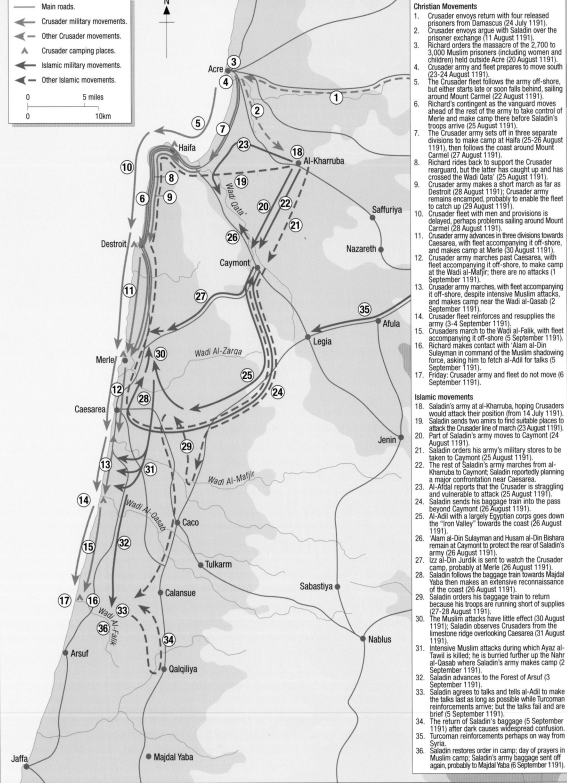

Legend

— Main roads.

⇐ Crusader military movements.

◁ Other Crusader movements.

▲ Crusader camping places.

⬅ Islamic military movements.

◁ Other Islamic movements.

0 — 5 miles
0 — 10km

N

Christian Movements

1. Crusader envoys return with four released prisoners from Damascus (24 July 1191).
2. Crusader envoys argue with Saladin over the prisoner exchange (11 August 1191).
3. Richard orders the massacre of the 2,700 to 3,000 Muslim prisoners (including women and children) held outside Acre (20 August 1191).
4. Crusader army and fleet prepares to move south (23-24 August 1191).
5. The Crusader fleet follows the army off-shore, but either starts late or soon falls behind, sailing around Mount Carmel (22 August 1191).
6. Richard's contingent as the vanguard moves ahead of the rest of the army to take control of Merle and make camp there before Saladin's troops arrive (25 August 1191).
7. The Crusader army sets off in three separate divisions to make camp at Haifa (25-26 August 1191), then follows the coast around Mount Carmel (27 August 1191).
8. Richard rides back to support the Crusader rearguard, but the latter has caught up and has crossed the Wadi Qata' (25 August 1191).
9. Crusader army makes a short march as far as Destroit (28 August 1191); Crusader army remains encamped, probably to enable the fleet to catch up (29 August 1191).
10. Crusader fleet with men and provisions is delayed, perhaps problems sailing around Mount Carmel (28 August 1191).
11. Crusader army advances in three divisions towards Caesarea, with fleet accompanying it off-shore, and makes camp at Merle (30 August 1191).
12. Crusader army marches past Caesarea, with fleet accompanying it off-shore, to make camp at the Wadi al-Mafjir; there are no attacks (1 September 1191).
13. Crusader army marches, with fleet accompanying it off-shore, despite intensive Muslim attacks, and makes camp near the Wadi al-Qasab (2 September 1191).
14. Crusader fleet reinforces and resupplies the army (3-4 September 1191).
15. Crusaders march to the Wadi al-Falik, with fleet accompanying it off-shore (5 September 1191).
16. Richard makes contact with 'Alam al-Din Sulayman in command of the Muslim shadowing force, asking him to fetch al-Adil for talks (5 September 1191).
17. Friday: Crusader army and fleet do not move (6 September 1191).

Islamic movements

18. Saladin's army at al-Kharruba, hoping Crusaders would attack their position (from 14 July 1191).
19. Saladin sends two amirs to find suitable places to attack the Crusader line of march (23 August 1191).
20. Part of Saladin's army moves to Caymont (24 August 1191).
21. Saladin orders his army's military stores to be taken to Caymont (25 August 1191).
22. The rest of Saladin's army marches from al-Kharruba to Caymont; Saladin reportedly planning a major confrontation near Caesarea.
23. Al-Afdal reports that the Crusader is straggling and vulnerable to attack (25 August 1191).
24. Saladin sends his baggage train into the pass beyond Caymont (26 August 1191).
25. Al-Adil with a largely Egyptian corps goes down the "Iron Valley" towards the coast (26 August 1191).
26. 'Alam al-Din Sulayman and Husam al-Din Bishara remain at Caymont to protect the rear of Saladin's army (26 August 1191).
27. Izz al-Din Jurdik is sent to watch the Crusader camp, probably at Merle (26 August 1191).
28. Saladin follows the baggage train towards Majdal Yaba then makes an extensive reconnaissance of the coast (26 August 1191).
29. Saladin orders his baggage train to return because his troops are running short of supplies (27-28 August 1191).
30. The Muslim attacks have little effect (30 August 1191); Saladin observes Crusaders from the limestone ridge overlooking Caesarea (31 August 1191).
31. Intensive Muslim attacks during which Ayaz al-Tawil is killed; he is buried further up the Nahr al-Qasab where Saladin's army makes camp (2 September 1191).
32. Saladin advances to the Forest of Arsuf (3 September 1191).
33. Saladin agrees to talks and tells al-Adil to make the talks last as long as possible while Turcoman reinforcements arrive; but the talks fail and are brief (5 September 1191).
34. The return of Saladin's baggage (5 September 1191) after dark causes widespread confusion.
35. Turcoman reinforcements perhaps on way from Syria.
36. Saladin restores order in camp; day of prayers in Muslim camp; Saladin's army baggage sent off again, probably to Majdal Yaba (6 September 1191).

Saladin's nephew Taqi al-Din tried to carve out a domain for himself in south-eastern Turkey during a crucial period of the Third Crusade. One of the most impressive fortresses in this mountainous region was Bitlis. (Author's photograph)

Having finally conquered Acre, the Crusader army marched south, passing through what is now the city of Haifa. (Author's photograph)

While Saladin's army shadowed them from the hills inland, the Crusaders clung to the coast, where possible stopping for the night around fortified places, like the now demolished castle of Destroit. (Author's photograph)

The Crusader army rested for some time outside the abandoned city of Caesarea after fighting off a determined attack by Saladin's army. (Author's photograph)

effectively destroying Saladin's navy. One of the two senior commanders in the city was allocated to King Philip for ransom, the other to Richard, and Saladin pulled most of his troops back to Shafr'amr, several kilometres along the road to Saffuriya. The garrison and population of Acre then filed out as the Crusaders entered the city. A quarrel erupted almost immediately when some of King Richard's soldiers threw Duke Leopold of Austria's banner from the walls, proclaiming that a mere duke should not display his flag alongside that of their victorious king. Leopold, of course, considered that he represented the German Empire.

Another part of the surrender terms was an exchange of prisoners, with Saladin also agreeing to pay a huge ransom for the garrison of Acre. The details of why this agreement failed are unknown but after Saladin released his first batch of prisoners on 24 July, there was a dispute over money. Meanwhile, the Crusader leaders decided that the Kingdom of

A galley with a lateen or triangular sail, as illustrated on an unusual fragment of glazed ceramic from Egypt, from around the time of Saladin's reign. (Museum of Islamic Art, Cairo; author's photograph)

Jerusalem should be divided in half, with the increasingly unpopular King Guy controlling Acre and any territory regained to the south, while Conrad of Monferrat retained Tyre and the north. Guy would also remain king until his death after which the crown would pass to Conrad or his descendants.

A few days later, on 31 July, King Philip Augustus started his journey home, though he left most of his troops behind. King Richard thus became the virtually undisputed commander of the entire Crusader army. On 11 August Crusader envoys reminded Saladin that the first handover of money and prisoners was due the next day. Ten thousand dinars and most of Saladin's 1,600 captives had been assembled, but arguments continued over Richard's release of the first batch of prisoners from Acre. Nine days later King Richard ordered that all of them, including wives, children and families be assembled and massacred. The only captives to be spared were a handful of high-value military and political leaders who were eventually ransomed the following year. The slaughter was witnessed by pickets from Saladin's army who tried to intervene but were easily beaten off.

In his letter to the Abbot of Clairvaux, Richard admitted that 'about 2,600' Saracens were 'quite properly' put to death, though 'a few of the more noble were spared, and we hoped to recover the Holy Cross and certain Christian captives in exchange for them.' It looked different from the other side as the chronicler Baha' al-Din wrote: 'The enemy then brought out the Muslim prisoners... about 3,000 bound in ropes. Then as one man they charged them and with stabbings and blows with the sword they slew them in cold blood, while the Muslim advance guard watched, not knowing what to do because they were at some distance from them.'[10] Only when Saladin sent reinforcements did the Muslims force the Crusaders back inside Acre, but by then the massacre was over.

THE MARCH TO ARSUF

An interesting aside in Baha' al-Din's account of these events states that two Bedouin had gone to Richard before he set out from Acre, informing him that Saladin's army was now so weak that the Crusaders could march south with ease. It soon became clear that this was what the Crusaders intended to do, so Saladin summoned a council of senior officers, then sent two *amirs* to identify suitable places where the enemy could be attacked. On 24 August he sent part of his army to establish a base at Caymont, at the foot of a pass across Mount Carmel. The following day the Crusader army began to move in three divisions, following the coastal road around Mount Carmel. The Crusader fleet had already set out, but was delayed by contrary winds and soon fell behind. Saladin responded by ordering his military stores to be taken to Caymont, though a great deal was abandoned at al-Kharruba through lack of transport. The division nominally commanded by Saladin's son al-Afdal remained close to the Crusader rearguard under the Duke of Burgundy, slowing it so that

INITIAL MOVEMENTS
(TO MID-MORNING, 7 SEPTEMBER 1191)

The Crusader army is in battle array facing inland but is also moving to its right, southwards. Saladin's army advances at an angle to the Crusader line of march, its right wing coming into contact with the Crusader 'left', which could be seen as its 'rear' in terms of its movement along the coast.

Note: Gridlines are shown at intervals of 1 kilometre

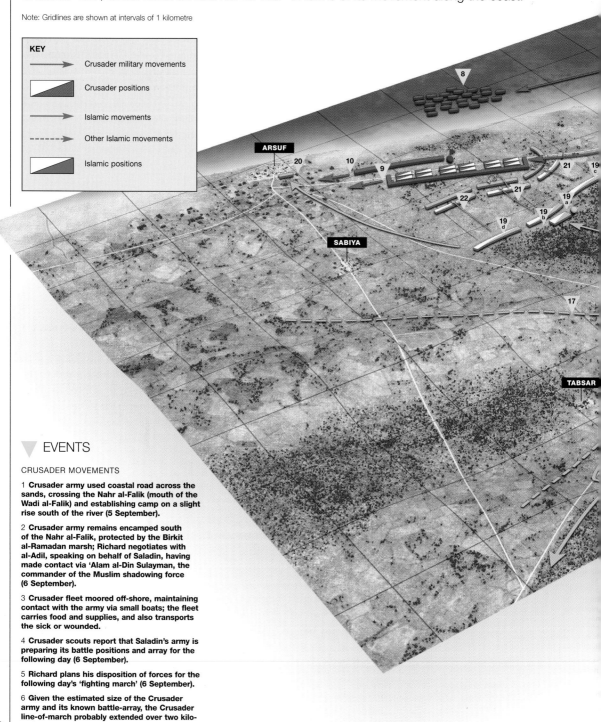

KEY

→ Crusader military movements

▱ Crusader positions

→ Islamic movements

--→ Other Islamic movements

◢ Islamic positions

ARSUF

SABIYA

TABSAR

▼ EVENTS

CRUSADER MOVEMENTS

1 Crusader army used coastal road across the sands, crossing the Nahr al-Falik (mouth of the Wadi al-Falik) and establishing camp on a slight rise south of the river (5 September).

2 Crusader army remains encamped south of the Nahr al-Falik, protected by the Birkit al-Ramadan marsh; Richard negotiates with al-Adil, speaking on behalf of Saladin, having made contact via 'Alam al-Din Sulayman, the commander of the Muslim shadowing force (6 September).

3 Crusader fleet moored off-shore, maintaining contact with the army via small boats; the fleet carries food and supplies, and also transports the sick or wounded.

4 Crusader scouts report that Saladin's army is preparing its battle positions and array for the following day (6 September).

5 Richard plans his disposition of forces for the following day's 'fighting march' (6 September).

6 Given the estimated size of the Crusader army and its known battle-array, the Crusader line-of-march probably extended over two kilometres or more.

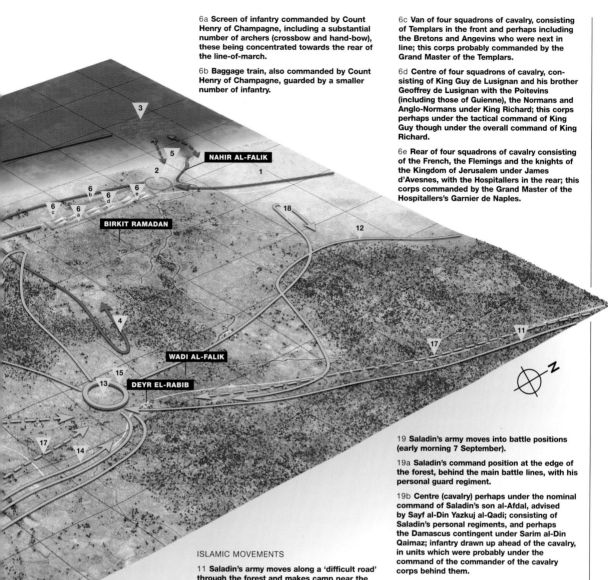

6a Screen of infantry commanded by Count Henry of Champagne, including a substantial number of archers (crossbow and hand-bow), these being concentrated towards the rear of the line-of-march.

6b Baggage train, also commanded by Count Henry of Champagne, guarded by a smaller number of infantry.

6c Van of four squadrons of cavalry, consisting of Templars in the front and perhaps including the Bretons and Angevins who were next in line; this corps probably commanded by the Grand Master of the Templars.

6d Centre of four squadrons of cavalry, consisting of King Guy de Lusignan and his brother Geoffrey de Lusignan with the Poitevins (including those of Guienne), the Normans and Anglo-Normans under King Richard; this corps perhaps under the tactical command of King Guy though under the overall command of King Richard.

6e Rear of four squadrons of cavalry consisting of the French, the Flemings and the knights of the Kingdom of Jerusalem under James d'Avesnes, with the Hospitallers in the rear; this corps commanded by the Grand Master of the Hospitallers's Garnier de Naples.

NAHIR AL-FALIK

BIRKIT RAMADAN

WADI AL-FALIK

DEYR EL-RABIB

ISLAMIC MOVEMENTS

11 Saladin's army moves along a 'difficult road' through the forest and makes camp near the village of Dayr al-Rabib at sunset (3 September).

12 A small force shadowing the Crusader army, commanded by 'Alam al-Din Sulayman.

13 Saladin's army remains in camp, resting, tending the wounded and reorganising; also unsuccessful negotiations are held between al-Adil and King Richard (4-5 September).

14 Saladin orders the heavy and light baggage trains, commanded by the Mir Akhur (Master of Horse) Aslam, to move south; Saladin then countermands all or part of this order; the light baggage and perhaps the heavy baggage returns to camp after dark, causing widespread confusion (5 September).

15 Saladin draws up battle plans for the following day with al-Adil (6 September).

16 Saladin definitively orders the baggage train (perhaps only the heavy baggage) to move to the vicinity of Majdal Yaba (6 September).

17 Local and bedouin volunteers continue to join Saladin's army; these are almost entirely infantry.

18 Saladin's scouts watch the Crusader camp and report Crusader movements.

Crusader army moves off shortly before dawn towards Arsuf in battle array, though moving sideways in terms of a traditional battle formation; Richard in the centre while Duke Hugues of Burgundy and an élite body of knights moves up and down the line-of-march, maintaining cohesion and ready to provide reinforcements where needed; the march is slow, to avoid gaps appearing between the divisions.

Crusader fleet sails parallel to the Crusader line-of-march.

Crusader vanguard reportedly approaching the 'orchards' of Arsuf by 9 am.

Some camp followers and part of the baggage train reportedly already starting to erect tents by 9 am.

19 Saladin's army moves into battle positions (early morning 7 September).

19a Saladin's command position at the edge of the forest, behind the main battle lines, with his personal guard regiment.

19b Centre (cavalry) perhaps under the nominal command of Saladin's son al-Afdal, advised by Sayf al-Din Yazkuj al-Qadi; consisting of Saladin's personal regiments, and perhaps the Damascus contingent under Sarim al-Din Qaimaz; infantry drawn up ahead of the cavalry, in units which were probably under the command of the commander of the cavalry corps behind them.

19c Right wing (cavalry) probably under the command of Saladin's brother al-Adil; largely consisting of the contingents from Egypt; infantry drawn up ahead of the cavalry, in units which were probably under the command of the commander of the cavalry corps behind them; 'Nubians' probably on the right, forming part of the largely Egyptian corps.

19d Left wing (cavalry); perhaps largely consisting of the contingents from the Jazira region and northern Iraq under the command of Ala al-Din Ibn 'Izz al-Din of Mosul; infantry drawn up ahead of the cavalry, in units which were probably under the command of the commander of the cavalry corps behind them.

20 Almost certainly some military presence in the abandoned town of Arsuf, though it is possible that Saladin sent reinforcements to Arsuf early in the day.

21 Infantry engage the enemy with bows and javelins from a distance; cavalry skirmishers make repeated horse-archery attacks but do not come to close combat.

22 It is unclear whether the left wing's infantry and skirmishers made much contact before the Crusader counter-charge was launched.

a gap opened up between this rearguard and the rest of the Crusader army on 25–26 August. But Saladin's main force was now moving towards Caymont and could not exploit this gap.

Saladin may have hoped to reach the coast ahead of the Crusaders, but King Richard led a fast-moving advance guard which established a strong position at Merle before their enemy arrived. Richard then hurried back to support the rearguard which now crossed the river Kishon to regain contact with the rest of the army. These first moves went in Richard's favour. Meanwhile, Saladin apparently decided on a major confrontation near Caesarea. On 26 August he accompanied the baggage train across the pass, but instead of descending to the coastal plain it followed the foothills towards Majdal Yaba (Mirabel). Al-Adil, with a largely Egyptian corps, went down to the narrow coastal strip while other contingents remained at Caymont in case part of the Crusader army attacked along the north-eastern slopes of Mount Carmel. A final contingent was sent to watch the Crusader vanguard at Merle.

David beheading Goliath in a late 12th-century English manuscript. The Philistine giant wears the best and most abundant armour available at this time. (*The Great Canterbury Psalter*, Bib. Nat., Ms. Lat. 8846, f. 2v., Paris)

This ability to disperse and re-assemble separate corps was typical of medieval Islamic armies and gave Saladin a clear strategic advantage, but because the Crusader army was moving so slowly Saladin ordered the baggage train to return. Apparently his forces were running short of supplies and so, paradoxically, the Crusaders' limited strategic manoeuvrability was turned to their advantage while Saladin's troops tired themselves hurrying to and fro. Finally, on Friday 30 August, the Crusaders advanced in three divisions towards Caesarea with their fleet accompanying them offshore.

Geoffrey de Lusignan commanded the vanguard, King Richard the centre, and the Duke of Burgundy the rearguard. Although Saladin had selected this part of the road for a major assault, the Muslim attacks had

The battlefield of Arsuf seen from the coastal dunes, looking south-eastward towards the low, wooded hills from which Saladin launched his attack. (Author's photograph)

Much of the coast between Caesarea and Arsuf is lined with sand dunes but there is often a cliff between the beach and the dunes, as seen here at the northern end of the Arsuf battlefield. (Author's photograph)

little effect and their main effort was harassment from a distance – which failed. As a result the Crusader army camped at the mouth of the Zarqa River, six kilometres (nearly four miles) north of Caesarea after a day of heat, dust, thirst and many wounded, but never having been seriously in danger of defeat. The following day both armies rested and watched each other. On 1 September the Crusaders marched a short distance to camp at the Nahr al-Mafjir, but were not challenged.

It was different on 2 September, as Baha' al-Din wrote: 'I saw various individuals amongst the Franks with ten arrows fixed in their backs, pressing on in this fashion quite unconcerned.' As they grew tired, those on the eastern flank of the Crusader line of march, facing these attacks, were alternated with those on the western or seaward side. Meanwhile, 'Their banner … proceeded in their midst on wheels like a huge beacon.' Later in the day, 'The Muslims were shooting arrows on their flanks, trying to incite them to break ranks, while they controlled themselves severely and covered the route in this way, travelling very steadily as their ships moved along at sea opposite them, until they completed each stage and camped. Their stages were short ones for the sake of the foot soldiers. Those resting were carrying the baggage and tents because they were short of beasts of burden.'[11]

This time Saladin's men attacked the enemy hand to hand, inflicting serious casualties but also suffering notable losses. Amongst those who fell was a renowned warrior named Ayaz al-Tawil, Ayaz the Tall, who was buried next to the Wadi al-Qasab where Saladin's army made camp. The

59

THE DEATH OF AYAZ AL-TAWIL (pages 60–61)

On Monday 2 September, Saladin's army made a concerted attack on the Crusader army as the latter marched along the coast. Unlike the battle of Arsuf a few days later, this was prolonged and determined harrassment rather than an all-out assault. It took place between the mouths of the Wadi al-Mafjir and the Wadi al-Qasab streams. Heavy casualties were suffered by both sides, and one incident caught the attention of both Muslim and Christian chroniclers.

This was the death of Ayaz al-Tawil – Ayaz the Tall (1). He was a big man, noted for his heavy armour and for a massive spear. The Crusaders (2) took this weapon (3) as a souvenir and they must have captured, or at least had time to exchange words, with Ayaz or one of the mamluks (4) who fought by his side. The Crusader chronicler Ambroise wrote than the famous weapon was called Ayaz Estog, which may be a garbled version of Ayaz Sungu, or 'Ayaz's spear' in medieval Turkish. Ayaz was buried with due ceremony when Saladin's army made camp further up the Wadi al-Qasab. (Christa Hook)

TOP **The cliffs which separated the battlefield at Arsuf from the sea are slightly higher here, at the town of Arsuf itself. (Author's photograph)**

RIGHT **There were substantial Christian minorities in most parts of Saladin's vast domain. Here the Church of Mar Hudeni in Mosul includes carvings reflecting the life of the Turkish ruling elite. (Author's photograph)**

RICHARD'S COUNTER-ATTACK (MID-MORNING, 7 SEPTEMBER 1191)

The first Crusade charge or counter-attack is often regarded as almost an unplanned accident. It certainly caught Saladin's troops by surprise and almost led to complete victory but the Muslims quickly rallied.

Note: Gridlines are shown at intervals of 1 kilometre

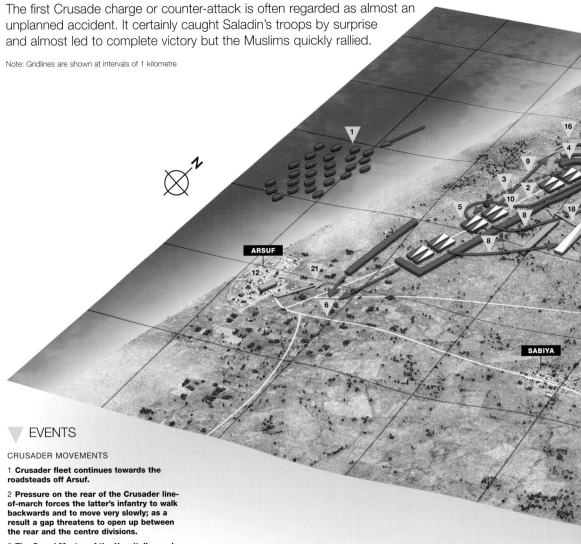

▼ EVENTS

CRUSADER MOVEMENTS

1 Crusader fleet continues towards the roadsteads off Arsuf.

2 Pressure on the rear of the Crusader line-of-march forces the latter's infantry to walk backwards and to move very slowly; as a result a gap threatens to open up between the rear and the centre divisions.

3 The Grand Master of the Hospitallers asks King Richard for permission to launch a counter-charge to remove the enemy pressure; this is turned down at least twice, the final request being made by the Grand Master in person.

4 Some Crusader infantry move to the area between the line-of-march and the coast, reportedly 'seeking refuge' but probably to counter the threat of the rear division being outflanked.

5 Richard prepares the cavalry to launch a coordinated counter-charge by the rear, centre and van divisions.

6 Part of the Cusader van, probably infantry, and perhaps the baggage train enter the orchards of Arsuf before the first Crusader counter-charge is launched.

7 Pressure on the rear of the line-of-march is so intense that cohesion was probably collapsing, so the Marshal of the Hospitallers starts a counter-charge without the authority of the Grand Master or King Richard; the

French who form the other part of the rear division cavalry immediately follow the Hospitallers' charge; Crusader infantry of the rear division do not have time to move aside and are thrown into confusion by this sudden charge.

8 As soon as the rear division launches its marginally premature charge, Richard orders the cavalry of the van to charge the enemy's left, then the centre to charge the enemy's centre; the infantry of the Crusader van and centre move aside to allow the cavalry through.

9 Some cavalry from the centre, including the squadron led by the Earl of Leicester, charge 'towards the sea', presumably against the enemy who have threatened to outflank the line-of-march; note that the Norman and Anglo-Norman squadrons who guard Richard's banner do not charge.

10 Richard and his immediate retinue charge in support of the Hospitallers, who may already have become disorganised and vulnerable.

ISLAMIC MOVEMENTS

11 Saladin's base-camp still occupied by support services, etc.; probably also protect by some troops.

12 There was almost certainly some Islamic military presence in Arsuf before the battle began.

13 The main cavalry units advance behind t infantry and cavalry skirmishers who have been harrassing the Crusader army for som time.

14 Saladin moves forward with the main forces, initially with only a handful of servar while his guard regiment remains in place a a reserve.

15 The main cavalry forces pass through the infantry and skirmishers who move aside for them, and close with the enemy in hand-to-hand combat; the main effort is directed against the Crusaders' rear division in an attempt to separate it from the centre and v

KEY

Crusader military movements

Crusader positions

Islamic military movements

Other Islamic movements

Islamic positions

BIRKIT RAMADAN

11

19

7

19

19

20

An attempt is also made to outflank the
[enem]y by getting between its line-of-march and
[th]e sea; the latter move perhaps hindered
[by] a small area of marshy ground; they make
[th]ree charges before the Hospitallers'
[un]authorised counter-charge.

Most of Saladin's guard regiment joins the
[m]ain attack, leaving the banners, drummers,
[et]c., with a small guard.

It is unclear whether the left flank makes
[m]uch contact before the Crusader counter-
[ch]arge.

19 The entire army withdraws to the shelter
of the forest; the right in disarray; the centre
and left in less disarray; the greatest losses
are suffered by the infantry and by those
horse-archers who have dismounted to take
better aim.

20 Saladin takes his headquarters team,
including flag-bearers, drummers, etc., to a
small hill in the forest; perhaps the tal later
known as Khirbat al-Jayus.

21 Some Muslim troops get between the
Crusaders' vanguard and Arsuf; these
probably being from Arsuf itself.

65

Crusaders meanwhile camped further downstream where the Qasab met the sea. The Muslims also took several prisoners whom Saladin interrogated and then had executed in retaliation for the massacre outside Acre. On 3 September King Richard remained in camp while Saladin broke off contact and, at midday according to Baha' al-Din, 'The drum was beaten and all moved off. The sultan entered the wooded area around Arsuf, into the very middle of it, as far as a hill near which was a village called Dayr al-Rabib, where he camped. Nightfall came upon us and our men were left scattered amongst the woods.' Many did not reach camp before nightfall and the army only re-assembled the following morning. Saladin then 'rode out to scout for a site suitable for a battle'.[12]

Meanwhile al-Adil was ordered to prolong the talking for as long as possible because Saladin expected the imminent arrival of Turkoman reinforcements, but this time al-Adil's temper got the better of him and his talks with King Richard's representatives were brief. On 5 September Richard took his army 14km (9 miles) south to the Nahr al-Falik where they remained encamped throughout the following day. According to Baha' al-Din, Richard also ordered the execution of the two Bedouin who had led him to believe that Saladin's army no longer posed a threat. On the other side, Saladin's previous attempts to contain the Crusader threat had failed and his army's morale might have been weakening. At first Saladin ordered the heavy baggage train to move further south, followed by the light baggage, but he changed his mind and ordered the baggage train to return. This it did after dark, causing considerable confusion, but next day Saladin restored order and, when his scouts reported that the

The early Islamic and early Crusader period fortifications of Arsuf remain virtually unchanged in the south-western corner of the town. (Author's photograph)

A horseman apparently trying to tether his reluctant horse to a tree, on the facade of a northern Italian church. (*In situ* Cathedral of San Donnino, Fidenza; author's photograph)

enemy were preparing to march the following morning, he decided to fight and sent the baggage away once again.

THE BATTLE OF ARSUF

King Richard was apparently aware that Saladin would make another serious attempt to stop the Crusader march on 7 September. His own preparations were very careful and we know a lot about his dispositions. These are most easily understood if seen as an army in battle array, facing inland (eastwards) with its back to the sea. This array then moved to its right, forming a line of march while anticipating attack against its 'front'. An outer screen of infantry, covering 'front' and 'flanks', was commanded by Henry of Champagne. He was also in charge of the Crusaders' baggage train in the 'rear' of the array, between the army and the coast. The 'centre' and 'wings' each had four cavalry squadrons. The 'centre' consisted of the men of Poitou and Guienne under King Guy and his brother Geoffrey de Lusignan, plus the Normans and Anglo-Normans under Richard himself. Although Richard was in command of the army, it is possible that Guy had tactical control of this 'central' division. The 'right wing', at the head of the crusader line of march, consisted of the Templars plus probably the Bretons and men from Anjou. It was commanded by the Grand Master of the Templars, probably Robert de Sablé who was elected in 1191, replacing Gerard de Ridefort who had been killed in 1189. The 'left wing', at the rear of the line of march, consisted of the French, the Flemings, the knights of the Kingdom of Jerusalem under James d'Avesnes and the Hospitallers, all

KING RICHARD HALTS THE CRUSADER CAVALRY'S COUNTER-ATTACK BECAUSE HE FEARS THE CRUSADERS WILL BE AMBUSHED. (pages 68–69)

King Richard (1) demonstrated his caution as a commander, as well as his courage as a warrior, at the battle of Arsuf. The initial Crusader counter-attack was launched a few minutes before Richard intended, but he seized the moment and sent Saladin's army (2) reeling back. He then regained control of his excited troops (3) and stopped them from pursuing the enemy into an area of low wooded hills where he feared an ambush. On the other side Saladin showed his powers as a commander by regaining control of his almost panic-stricken men and getting them to make a stand. This would be repeated twice during the course of the battle, though not as dramatically as the first time. By the end of the battle Richard had achieved a victory, albeit a partial one, while Saladin had avoided what might have turned into a catastrophic defeat. (Christa Hook)

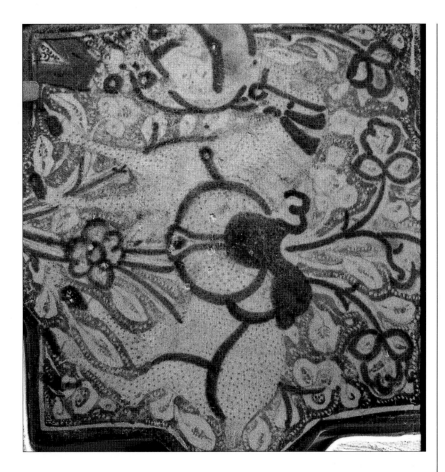

under the command of Garnier de Naples the Grand Master of the Hospitallers. In both the right and left flanks the elite brethren of the Military Orders, Templars and Hospitallers, formed the outer ranks.

According to Baha' al-Din, when Saladin heard that the enemy was breaking camp he drew up his own men in array. Since they had to pass through a forested area before reaching their chosen battleground, the arraying was probably done after they emerged into the open terrain beyond. The Crusader Ambroise described Taqi al-Din's banner in great, if rather misleading detail, but the Islamic sources make no mention of Taqi al-Din, who is unlikely to have been present at the battle of Arsuf. Perhaps this yellow banner was carried by Saladin's own elite corps, or the unit commanded by his renowned *mamluk* Sarim al-Din Qaymaz al-Najmi, or was the flag of al-Adil's corps.

No specific description of Saladin's battle array survives, but the following reconstruction is based upon what happened during the course of the battle. Saladin himself selected a command position behind the main array. Ahead of him the centre was probably under the nominal command of his son al-Afdal, advised by the older Sayf al-Din Yazkuj al-Qadi with the Syrian contingents. The Damascus contingent under Sarim al-Din Qaymaz may have been attached to the centre, or may have formed part of Saladin's own guard. The right wing seems to have been commanded by Saladin's brother al-Adil. The left wing may have consisted of northern contingents from the Jazira and northern Iraq commanded by Ala al-Din Ibn 'Izz al-Din of Mosul.

THE LATER PHASES OF THE BATTLE (MID-MORNING 7 SEPTEMBER TO 8 SEPTEMBER 1191)

There were several Crusader charges and Islamic counter-charges during the course of the battle which concluded with a partial success for King Richard's army.

Note: Gridlines are shown at intervals of 1 kilometre

ARSUF

SABIYA

▼ EVENTS

CRUSADER MOVEMENTS

1 **Crusader fleet probably sails south of Arsuf before anchoring in support of the Crusader army's encampment.**

2 **Much of the Crusader infantry advances in support of the cavalry, killing wounded Muslim troops as they went.**

3 **A contingent commanded by the Earl of Leicester, perhaps with the contingent of Count Robert of Dreux and the Bishop of Dreux, cuts off part of the right wing of Saladin's army.**

4 **Norman and Anglo-Norman cavalry with Richard's banner advance slowly and stop at a distance from the fighting to establish a rallying position for the rest of the Crusader army.**

5 **The Crusader rear disperses part of the Islamic right wing and forces the rest of it back into the forest after hard fighting; so much dust is thrown up, hampering visibility, that the knights sometimes attack their own men, probably the disorganised infantry which has advanced with them.**

6 **The Crusader centre pursues the retreating Islamic centre into the forest, but only makes slight contact with the enemy cavalry.**

7 **The Crusader van (now their right wing) pursues the retreating Islamic left wing into the forest but does not apparently make contact with the enemy cavalry.**

8 **Fearing ambushes in the forest, the Crusader cavalry withdraws towards the safety of its infantry but suffers casualties from an immediate Islamic counter-attack.**

9 **Death of James d'Avesnes at the northern end of the battlefield.**

10 **Crusader cavalry reassembles behind the shelter of its infantry; then counter-charges a second and a third time.**

11 **Richard and William des Barres lead their squadrons to defeat a dangerous Muslim cavalry counter-attack against the Crusaders' left flank (previously the rear of their line-of-march).**

12 **Crusader baggage train, presumably protected by some infantry, continues to march south and establishes a camp in the 'orchards' south of Arsuf; probably in a location with available water supplies.**

13 **Crusader army breaks off combat about mid-day and moves towards the camp which is already being established south of Arsuf; taking their dead and wounded with them.**

14 **Richard makes a final charge with a small troop of cavalry, forcing the 'garrison' of Arsuf back into the abandoned town.**

15 **Many Crusader scavengers return to the battlefield the following night (7-8 September) to plunder the dead; they find the Muslims collecting their dead and wounded.**

16 **The Crusaders do not respond to Saladin's demonstration (8 September) and remain encamped south of Arsuf (until 9 September).**

ISLAMIC MOVEMENTS

17 **Part of the right wing are cut off by the Earl of Leicester's charge and attempt to escape along the beach or by swimming.**

18 **Saladin fears that his army has been routed; he re-establishes his headquarters o a hill (tal) in the forest and rallies his troops using banners and drums.**

19 **Islamic infantry thrown into disorder, retreats into the forest or flees the battlefiel altogether; all divisions probably suffer casualties, those on the right wing being particularly heavy; the infantry who reach th forest start to fight back as soon as they hav the cover of the trees.**

20 **Muslims counter-attack with bows and javelins as soon as the Crusader cavalry beg to withdraw; the counter-attack is repeated after the second Crusader cavalry charge bu not after the third, leaving the Crusaders in control of the battlefield until they withdraw.**

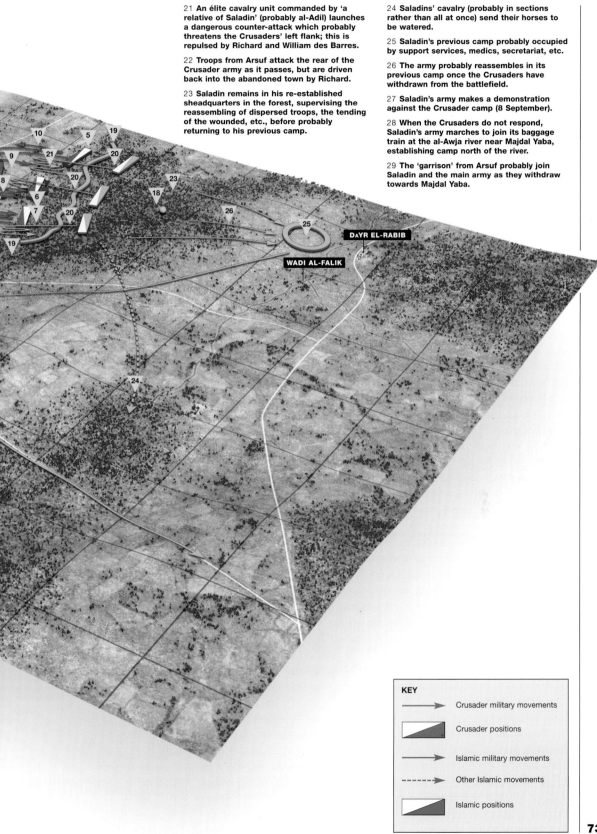

21 An élite cavalry unit commanded by 'a relative of Saladin' (probably al-Adil) launches a dangerous counter-attack which probably threatens the Crusaders' left flank; this is repulsed by Richard and William des Barres.

22 Troops from Arsuf attack the rear of the Crusader army as it passes, but are driven back into the abandoned town by Richard.

23 Saladin remains in his re-established sheadquarters in the forest, supervising the reassembling of dispersed troops, the tending of the wounded, etc., before probably returning to his previous camp.

24 Saladins' cavalry (probably in sections rather than all at once) send their horses to be watered.

25 Saladin's previous camp probably occupied by support services, medics, secretariat, etc.

26 The army probably reassembles in its previous camp once the Crusaders have withdrawn from the battlefield.

27 Saladin's army makes a demonstration against the Crusader camp (8 September).

28 When the Crusaders do not respond, Saladin's army marches to join its baggage train at the al-Awja river near Majdal Yaba, establishing camp north of the river.

29 The 'garrison' from Arsuf probably join Saladin and the main army as they withdraw towards Majdal Yaba.

DAYR EL-RABIB

WADI AL-FALIK

KEY

→ Crusader military movements

◢ Crusader positions

→ Islamic military movements

---→ Other Islamic movements

◢ Islamic positions

Infantry units were drawn up in front of each division, under the tactical command of the cavalry corps behind them and probably being drawn from regions associated with those cavalry. Hence the so-called Nubian infantry are likely to have been on the right, ahead of al-Adil's troops from Egypt. Saladin also had troops in the abandoned fortified city of Arsuf, though it is unclear how long they had been there.

Shortly before dawn on 7 September 1191, Richard's army left its camp on a small hill next to the Nahr al-Falik and marched slowly south, along a rise which lies between the beach and the low-lying, partially agricultural land. Beyond this shallow depression rose the low hills of the Forest of Arsuf. The Crusaders marched for several hours and their column stretched over a considerable distance. Around 9 o'clock in the morning the left wing was approaching orchards and gardens which surrounded Arsuf. By this time Saladin's army had arrayed itself in front of the forest and the sultan may have been awaiting this moment of *nuzul* to attack (see previous chapter, *Opposing Plans*); perhaps hoping the leading part of the enemy army would hurry forward while his own troops attacked and slowed down the rear of its column – thus opening a gap in the enemy line.

This gruesome scene of massacre is in a small country church in Central Italy. The armour appears primitive, with the soldier wearing an apparently sleeveless mail hauberk. (*In situ* Church of Santa Maria Ronzano, Castel Castagna

Two detailed and colourful accounts of Saladin's initial attack survive, written by men who were there, though on opposing sides. According to Baha' al-Din, the sultan, 'sent forward a picked body of skirmishers from each division. The enemy marched on until they were close to the woods and plantations of Arsuf. The skirmishers loosed their arrows against them and then the divisions pressed them close from every direction. The sultan made them engage closely, but held some back in reserve… Amongst the enemy there were dead and wounded and they quickened their march in the hope of reaching the site where they would camp. Their situation became serious and the noose about them tightened, while the sultan was moving between the left wing and the right wing, urging the men on to the *jihad*. Several times I encountered him, when he was attended by only two pages with two spare mounts and that was all. I met his brother in a similar state, while the arrows were flying past them both.' Ibn al-Athir added that the head of the thirsty Crusader column was close to a source of drinking water when the battle began, and that some were pushed back so far that they had to jump into the sea, though this is probably an exaggeration.

The anonymous Crusader author of the *Itinerarium* obtains most of his information from the poet Ambroise. He wrote, 'As the third hour approached the huge Turkish multitude – around 10,000 of them [a huge exaggeration] – came charging down on our people at swift gallop! With a confusion of cries they eagerly threw javelins and shot arrows, making a terrifying din. After these ran a devilish race, very black in colour, who for this reason have an appropriate name; because they are black [*nigri*] they are called Negroes. Also there were the Saracens who travel about in the desert, popularly called Bedouins; savage and darker than soot, the most redoubtable infantrymen, carrying bows and quivers and round shields. They are a very energetic and agile people. These threatened our army constantly without giving way. Beyond these you would have seen the serried ranks of Turks approaching across open country. They were well drawn up with so many emblems fixed to their lances, so many standards, so many banners with a variety of details, so many lines appropriately divided into troops and troops arranged in companies that there seemed at a guess to be more than 20,000 armed Turks [another exaggeration] approaching in order... Certain people were assigned to go before the amirs sounding trumpets and clarions; others held horns, others flutes, tambourines, rattles or cymbals, others had other instruments for making a noise. They were assigned to the single task of raising shouts and horrible yells.'[13]

These attacks were initially in the form of skirmishing from a distance with bows and javelins, and it is unclear whether the left wing or even the centre of Saladin's army yet made much contact with the enemy. This may again have been intentional, as the head of the Crusader column, or at least the head of the baggage column, had already started to erect tents when the battle reached its climax. Meanwhile, pressure on the left wing or rear of the Crusader column meant that many infantrymen had to walk backwards so that they could fight Saladin's troops. This inevitably slowed their progress, further weakening the link between the left wing and the centre. Other foot soldiers reportedly 'sought refuge' between the line of march and the coast, though they probably moved to this area to stop the army being outflanked.

More than once the Grand Master of the Hospitallers sent messengers to Richard, asking permission to launch a countercharge because so many horses were being killed or wounded. Fatalities amongst the armoured men were few, but many suffered injury. Finally the Grand Master rode up to the King in person, but again his request was denied because Richard was preparing a co-ordinated charge by the entire Crusader cavalry force. By now part of Saladin's infantry had drawn aside, enabling the Muslim cavalry to attack. As they came into close combat, it became virtually impossible for the Crusader left wing to march, though they attempted to do so. For the mounted knights this was humiliating as well as dangerous as it meant turning their backs on the enemy. It may have been now that Saladin sent his guard contingent, perhaps including Sarim al-Din Qaymaz's regiment, into the fray, leaving himself with only drummers, messengers and a handful of followers.

All Crusader sources agree it was at this point the Marshal of the Hospitallers could stand the strain no longer and launched his 'unauthorized' charge. Closer study of the events, and of the tactical role expected of a Marshal of one of the Military Orders, strongly suggests that his actions were misunderstood at the time, and have been misrepresented ever since. Certainly Baha' al-Din, who witnessed what happened, believed that the Crusader actions were well planned, superbly timed and well co-ordinated.

What can be said with confidence is that pressure on the Hospitallers and French in the Crusader left wing or rear became so intense that their cohesion began to fragment. The noise was also such that the Marshal

may have thought he heard the trumpet blasts with which King Richard would signal a co-ordinated charge. Nor is it entirely clear whether the Hospitaller Grand Master had yet returned from speaking with Richard. Did the Marshal take the initiative or did he think the trumpet had sounded? Certainly a brother knight of his status and experience would not have lost his head and simply attacked the nearest foe. Whatever the precise cause, the result was dramatic and successful. Somehow it also sounds better in the medieval French of King Richard's dedicated follower, the poet Ambroise (*see footnote for translation*):

> L'un des deus fud uns chevaliers,
> Li mareschals ospitaliers;
> L'autre iert Baudowins li Carons,
> Qui iert hardiz com uns leons:
> Compainz iert le rei d'Engleterre,
> Qui l'ot amené de sa terre.
> Cist commencerent le desrei
> El saint non del tot poissant rei;
> Saint Jorge a haute voiz crierent!
> E les genz Dampnedeu tornerent
> Lor chevals ço davant dariere
> Encontre la cruel gent fiere.[14]

TOP LEFT **The single-edged, curved sabre of Turkish Central Asian origin had already been adopted by some Middle Eastern troops and appears in this 12th-century ceramic bowl from Iran. (Museum of Oriental Art, Rome; author's photograph)**

TOP RIGHT **Attendant guards were also used as decorative motifs in Islamic metalwork made around the time of Saladin, including this bronze strongbox, probably from northern Iraq. (Museum of Fine Arts, Boston; author's photograph)**

This charge was so sudden that the Crusader infantry of the left wing failed to move out of its way and were thrown into confusion. King Richard, in his later letter to the Abbot of Clairvaux, merely stated: 'Our vanguard was proceeding and was already setting up camp at Arsuf, when Saladin and his Saracens made a violent attack on our rearguard,

Crusader Movements
1. Crusaders camp at Arsuf (8 September 1191).
2. Crusaders march to Jaffa, with fleet off-shore (9-10 September 1191).
3. Geoffrey de Lusignan sails to Ascalon then reports demolition to Richard.
4. Richard sends Humphrey of Toron to al-Adil to discuss peace, nothing is agreed (October 1191).
5. Renaud of Sidon arrives in Saladin's camp as ambassador from Conrad of Monferrat (5 November 1191).
6. Richard leads Crusader army to take Ramla (22 November 1191); occupies Lydda (25 December 1191); advances to Bayt Nuba (3 January 1191).
7. Richard orders retreat (8 January 1191).
8. Crusader Council (20 January 1192) agrees that Richard rebuilds fortifications of Ascalon.
9. Fighting in Acre between Pisans and Genoese.
10. Richard returns to Acre (20 February 1192) and arranges a truce between Pisans and Genoese; Crusader leaders decide Conrad of Monferrat should replace Guy as King.
11. Negotiations restart between Richard and al-Adil.
12. Conrad of Monferrat assassinated in Tyre (28 April 1192); Henry of Champagne marries Conrad's widow Isabella and is crowned King.
13. News arrives from England that Prince John is usurping power (April 1192).
14. Richard abandons peace negotiations and attacks Darum (taken on 23 May 1192).
15. Crusaders march against Bayt Nuba (11 June 1192).
16. Richard attacks and captures the Egyptian caravan at Khuwaylifa (23 June 1192).
17. Crusaders return with booty (29 June 1192).
18. Crusaders withdraw to Ramla (4-5 July 1192).
19. Richard asks Saladin for negotiations (9 July 1192) then travels to Acre.
20. Richard lands at Jaffa and forces back Saladin's troops (31 July – 1 August 1192); army from Acre reaches Caesarea (3 August 1192).
21. Crusaders sign peace agreement (2 September 1192).
22. Queen Berengaria and Queen Joanna sail from Acre (29 September 1192); Richard sails from Acre (October 1192).

Islamic Movements
23. Saladin makes a demonstration against the Crusader camp (8 September 1191).
24. Skimishers try to provoke Crusaders into an ambush (9 September 1191); Saladin sends army to Ramla (10 September 1191).
25. Saladin goes to Ascalon to supervise demolition (10-11 September 1191).
26. Saladin goes to Ramla (23 September 1191), orders the demolition of the castle then inspects the defences of Jerusalem.
27. Saladin pulls army back to Latrun.
28. Saladin opens negotiations with Conrad of Monferrat (early November 1191).
29. Saladin summons council to discuss peace proposals from Richard and Conrad (11 November 1191) then pulls back to Latrun (17 November 1191).

30. Saladin disbands most of his army and takes remainder to Jerusalem (12 December 1191).
31. Muslim unit attacks Crusader outposts (29 December 1191 - 3 January 1192).
32. Army from Egypt camps outside Jerusalem (22 January 1192).
33. Izz al-Din Jurdik raids Yubna (28 January 1192).
34. Masons arrive from Mosul.
35. Al-Afdal leaves for Syria (February 1192).
36. Izz al-Din Jurdik raids outskirts of Ascalon (18 February 1192).
37. Faris al-Din Maimun raids Yubna and Jaffa (1 March 1192).
38. Al-Adil sent with troops to Baisan (20 March 1192) to negotiate peace with King Richard's representatives.
39. In mid-May al-Adil is sent to the Jazira to settle affairs there.
40. Turcoman reinforcements reach Jerusalem (31 May 1192).
41. Saladin sends small force under the Mir Akhur Aslam to warn the caravan from Egypt (22 June 1192).
42. Large supply caravan is attacked by Richard's force (24 June 1192).
43. Saladin watches Crusaders retreat to the coast (4 July 1192).
44. Al-Afdal and al-Zahir return to Jerusalem with their armies (2-17 July 1192).
45. Saladin camps between Lydda and Ramla (25 July 1192); unsuccessful siege of Jaffa (27-31 July 1192); Saladin resumes talks with Richard (1 August 1192).
46. Contingents from Jazira and Iraq (23 July 1192) are sent to Baisan, under Mujahid al-Din Yurun-qush.
47. Saladin marches against Crusader army approaching from Acre, then makes a sudden but unsuccessful attack on Richard outside Jaffa (4 August 1192).
48. Saladin withdraws to Latrun (5 August 1192).
49. Mosul contingent arrives from Marj Ayun (5 August 1192).
50. Reinforcements reach Saladin from Egypt (20 August 1192).
51. Saladin makes probing attack to Jaffa then sends peace offer (28 August 1192).
52. Saladin returns to Latrun and disbands most of his army (5-10 September 1192); Saladin remains in Jerusalem until Richard leaves Acre, then goes to Damascus.
53. Muslim contingent sent to demolish Ascalon, accompanied by a Crusader detachment (5 September 1192).

Main roads.
Saladin's main army moving between Bayt Nuba, Latrun & Ramla.
Islamic military movements.
Other Islamic movements.
Crusader military movements.
Other Crusader movements.
Joint Crusader & Islamic mission to demolish the fortifications of Ascalon.

0   10 miles
0   20km

An Islamic sailing ship on a ceramic bowl, probably made in Tunisia in the 12th century. (Museo Nazionale San Matteo, Pisa)

but by the grace of God's favourable mercy they were forced into flight just by the four squadrons that were facing them.' Although Richard gave all the credit to the Hospitallers and French knights of the left wing, other sources add that the English king, seeing that the left had jumped the gun, immediately ordered the centre and right to charge. To what extent, if any, these divisions made contact with the enemy at this point is unclear. Richard and his own retinue then hurried to support the Hospitallers, though the Norman and Anglo-Norman knights who guarded the king's banner did not charge. Instead they followed slowly so that their banner formed a rallying point after the charge had ended. One or more further squadrons from the centre of the Crusader array, including that of the Earl of Leicester, charged in a different direction 'towards the sea', presumably against enemy troops who were threatening to outflank the Crusader line of march.

Baha' al-Din saw things from the other side: 'The enemy's situation worsened still more and the Muslims thought they had them in their power... Then their cavalry massed together and agreed on a charge, as they feared for their people and thought that only a charge would save them. I saw them grouped together in the middle of the foot soldiers. They took their lances and gave a shout as one man. The infantry opened gaps for them and they charged in unison along their whole line.' Part of

Saladin's array was already in close contact with the Crusaders' left wing. Elsewhere, and perhaps also here, many Muslim horsemen had dismounted in order to take careful aim at the enemy. As a result the sudden Crusader charge hit many Muslim contingents, especially the infantry, before they had a chance to escape, causing serious casualties and driving Saladin's army back in disorder.

Though the Crusaders did not realize it, Saladin's army was on the brink of rout as it fled towards the wooded hills. Saladin took his headquarters staff, flag-bearers and drummers to a small hill in the forest, probably to what was later known as Khirbat al-Jayus. Abu Shama made no attempt to disguise the Crusaders' success: 'The Franks charged furiously in a mass, knocking over and driving into flight the troops who were in front of them.' Baha' al-Din's account was more personal, 'One group charged our right wing, another our left and the third our centre. Our men gave way before them. It happened that I was in the centre, which took to wholesale flight. My intention was to join the left wing, since it was nearer to me. I reached it after it had been broken utterly, so I thought to join the right wing, but then I saw that it had fled more calamitously than all the rest. I determined to join the sultan's guard, which was in reserve to support all the others as was customary. I came to him, but the sultan had kept no more than 17 fighting men and had taken the rest into battle, but the standards were still flying and the drum was beating without interruption. When the sultan saw this reverse that had befallen the Muslims, he returned to his guard and found there this scanty number. He stood amongst them while men were fleeing on all sides, but he was commanding the drummers to beat their drums without stopping. He ordered me to rally to him all those he saw fleeing. However, the Muslims were, in truth, in a complete rout.'

Two later Arab chroniclers described the fate of the non-combatants who had gathered near the battle, perhaps part of the 'army bazaar' which habitually followed Islamic armies. According to Ibn al-Athir: 'Many riders and the ordinary people had as usual collected near the battlefield during the battle. This day they did as they usually did. When the Muslims took to flight, a great number of these people were killed.' Abu'l-Fida was a member of the Ayyubid dynasty, founded by Saladin, which ruled the Syrian city of Hama in the early 14th century and he may have been drawing upon a family tradition when he described the Crusaders 'reaching close to the place [close to the camp] where the market was held, they massacred there a multitude of small merchants and their customers.'

The Crusaders may not have reached the wooded area at the end of this first charge. Their cavalry now paused to re-assemble. Behind them the Crusader infantry also advanced, killing or capturing wounded or unhorsed enemy troops, but dust was already causing difficulty, as the *Itinerarium* explained, 'The jumble of combatants threw up the dust. This was very dangerous to our people, because when they were tired with the slaughter they might withdraw from the thick of the battle to catch their breath, but they could not recognize each other because of the great cloud of dust.' Meanwhile Saladin's disciplined army rallied and returned to the fight. To quote Ibn al-Athir, 'If the Franks had realised that this was a genuine rout they would have pursued further, the collapse would have continued and the Muslims would have been slaughtered. But there was in the vicinity a very dense forest which they entered. The Franks, imagining that this was a ruse of war, turned back, and the distress in which the Muslims had found themselves was ended.' Abu Shama and Imad al-Din both gave particular credit to al-Adil, Qaymaz al-Najmi and the troops of Mosul for 'holding firm'.

As the Crusaders pulled back, the Muslims attacked and, in the words of the *Itinerarium*: 'Without delay, more than 20,000 [again a huge exaggeration] of them set off in pursuit and rushed down on their [the withdrawing Crusaders'] rear as they went, brandishing very heavy maces in their hands in order to free those whom our people had thrown down. Then you would have seen our people being horribly thrashed! They also threw javelins and arrows at them as they fell back.' Crusader chroniclers maintain that Taqi al-Din led this counterattack, though al-Adil should probably be given credit.

After the Crusader cavalry re-assembled behind its infantry, it charged for the second time. King Richard now entered the thick of the fighting when he and William des Barres led their squadrons against the most threatening part of the Muslim line. James d'Avesnes, the most senior Crusader to die at the battle of Arsuf, was killed during this stage. As Baha' al-Din put it, 'Our men fled but fought as they fled. The enemy halted again, as did our men.' This time both sides reached the hills and found themselves in what Ibn al-Athir called 'a countryside of scrubby vegetation with many trees'.

Disaster again threatened but, according to Baha' al-Din, 'All who saw the sultan's troop holding its position with drums beating were ashamed to pass beyond it and feared the disaster which might follow, so they rallied to his troop and a large number assembled there. The enemy stood facing them on the tops of the hills and hillocks, while the sultan was with his troop and men were gathering round him. Eventually the whole army rallied and the enemy feared that there might be an ambush in the woods, so they withdrew, making for their camping place.'

Events now become less clear. The Crusaders fell back in good order and established camp near a source of drinking water south of Arsuf. At some point Saladin's troops in Arsuf attacked, either attempting to stop the Crusaders making camp, or perhaps wanting to avoid being trapped inside the abandoned city. This was almost certainly the point at which King Richard led a third and final charge, supposedly driving the garrison back into Arsuf, although Baha' al-Din maintains that the third Crusader charge 'brought them to the tops of some hillocks and a ridge of hills. Our troops fled again until the enemy halted and then they also halted.'

Abu Shama probably reflected a widespread belief held within Saladin's army that both sides had suffered great loss, and the death of James d'Avesnes – 'one of their chiefs who was killed' in Ibn al-Athir's words – was clearly a serious blow. However, King Richard reflected the attitudes of his class when he wrote to the Abbot of Clairvaux that, 'By the grace of God we lost no one that day except that best of men whose merits had made him dear to the whole army, James d'Avesnes.' No one, that is, except lesser members of society whose death was not worth mentioning. Muslim losses were certainly greater, though Richard was probably overstating the case when he estimated that, 'So great was the slaughter among Saladin's more noble Saracens, that he lost more that day near Arsuf – it was Sunday, the vigil of the nativity of the Blessed Virgin Mary – than on any day in the previous 40 years.'

Baha' al-Din provides a more personal account of the aftermath. 'The sultan', he wrote, 'went back to a hill where the woods began and halted there, but not in any tent. I was in attendance on him, offering consolation, which, however, he was unable to accept. He was protected from the sun by a kerchief and we asked him to take some food. Something light was brought to him, from which he took only a little. The troops sent their horses to be watered, for the source of water was far away. He sat waiting for people to return from watering their mounts, while the wounded were brought before him and he was giving orders for them to be treated and carried away. That day many foot-soldiers were killed and a lot on both sides were wounded. Amongst those who stood firm were al-Adil, the *tawashi* Qaymaz al-Najmi and al-Afdal, the sultan's son, who was shaken by this day. A boil that was on his face burst and much blood flowed over his face, but he was steadfast and confident of his future reward through all of this. The troops of Mosul with their commander, Ala al-Din, stood firm this day and the sultan thanked him for that. Our men enquired after one another and many of the army were found to have met a martyr's death, notable amongst whom were the *Amir Shikar* (Commander of the Hunt) Musak, who was a brave and well-known man, Qaymaz al-'Adili and Buzghush, brave men of note.'[15]

Scavengers from the Crusader camp returned to the battlefield during the night to plunder the dead. There they found the Muslims collecting their dead and wounded. No fighting was reported, so perhaps each concentrated on looking after their own. Next day Saladin's army drew up near the Crusader camp but did not attack, nor did King Richard's men respond. This was probably a demonstration to bolster Muslim morale, as Saladin, who was now seriously ill, then took his troops south, to rejoin their baggage train encamped on the northern side of the Awja River near Majdal Yaba.

No graves or grave-pits associated with the battle of Arsuf have yet been found. Nevertheless, recent studies of the skeletal remains found at Vadum Yaqub, which fell to Saladin's army 12 years earlier, provide shocking evidence of the reality of crusading warfare. There was, for example, a much higher proportion of blade injuries which amputated limbs or cut right through bones than have been found in excavations at European battle sites. Even when the question of armour, or a lack of it, is taken into consideration, the reasons for this phenomenon remain unclear. Furthermore, blade injuries to exposed areas like the face and forearms were unusually deep, perhaps reflecting the style and quality of Islamic blades or the fencing styles of those who wielded them.

The immediate results of the battle of Arsuf and the siege of Acre were summed up by the historians Lyons and Jackson. After these events, they wrote, 'if it was difficult for him [Saladin] to win, the Franks could still lose. They had scored an undoubted success, but the Muslim rout was, in fact, little more than an undignified and expensive version of their usual tactics… The Franks, however, had not been able to trap them and Saladin had rallied them successfully. He could expect reinforcements, and the Franks for their part suffered losses and would certainly find it difficult to replace their dead horses.'[16] In fact, the fall of Acre had been a more serious blow to Saladin than his setback outside Arsuf. It was a major strategic loss, and cost him many troops including members of elite regiments, plus a great deal of war *matériel* and virtually the entire naval fleet. Following on so closely after each other, the fall of Acre and the battle of Arsuf were also massive blows to Saladin's prestige.

11 Baha' al-Din Ibn Shaddad (tr. D.S. Richards), *The Rare and Excellent History of Saladin*, Aldershot (2002), pp.170–1.
12 Ibid,, pp.172-3.
13 Anon. (trans. K. Fenwick), *The Third Crusade*, London (1958), pp.247–8.
14 'One of these two was a (brother) knight, the Marshal of the Hospital, the other was Baudouin le Caron, who was as brave as a lion, a companion of the King of England who had brought him. The two began their attack with the name of the All Powerful and cried in a loud voice, St. George! The men of God then turned their horses against the enemy.' Ambroise (ed. & trans. G. Paris), *L'Estoire de la Guerre Sainte*, Paris (1897), pp.171–2.
15 Baha' al-Din Ibn Shaddad (tr. D.S. Richards), *The Rare and Excellent History of Saladin*, Aldershot (2002), pp.174–176.
16 M.C. Lyons & D.E.P. Jackson, *Saladin: The politics of the Holy War*, Cambridge (1982), p.338.

AFTERMATH

The war of manoeuvre now resumed, and, when the Crusader army marched south on 9 September, several *amirs* wanted to lure them into an ambush but the Crusaders did not respond so Saladin broke off contact. On the 10th Saladin consulted his senior commanders. Would the Crusaders now head for Jerusalem or for Ascalon where they could threaten Saladin's communications with Egypt? The Muslims did not have enough troops to defend both places so Saladin decided to demolish Ascalon and focus on Jerusalem. The following night he rode to Ascalon to supervise its demolition while al-Adil remained in Ramla to watch the Crusaders. The latter remained in Jaffa until 31 October, rebuilding it as a strong base which they would need if and when Richard advanced inland towards Jerusalem.

The sight of the inhabitants of Ascalon having to abandon their homes caused Saladin's illness to worsen, but it took several days for rumours of the demolition to reach Jaffa. When they did, Geoffrey de

After the battle of Arsuf, Saladin withdrew much of his army to Jerusalem. He also provided a magnificent wooden pulpit for the great al-Aqsa Mosque. Centuries later this was burned by an Australian fanatic, resulting in the scaffolding in the rear of this picture. (Author's photograph)

Lusignan sailed there to see what was happening and when he returned, King Richard wanted to march against Ascalon. However, the other leaders were unenthusiastic. On 23 September Saladin returned to Ramla, ordering that its castle also be demolished while the contents of government granaries in this part of Palestine were taken to Jerusalem.

The unsettled state of the northern borders of Saladin's realm were causing concern and would divert some of Saladin's attention, and even some troops, for many months. In fact Saladin had too much on his plate, and must have been glad when, early in October, King Richard sent Humphrey of Toron to meet al-Adil in Lydda to discuss a truce. No decisions were reached and there would be many efforts to negotiate before the Third Crusade spluttered to its unsatisfactory conclusion. In the meantime Saladin strengthened Jerusalem, pulled most of his troops back to Latrun, and established a base outside Ascalon.

The talking continued through October 1191. Initially Richard demanded all Palestine as far as the river Jordan and the return of the Holy Cross captured at the battle of Hattin. He suggested that Saladin's brother al-Adil become a Christian, or marry Richard's sister Queen Joanna of Sicily, when they could jointly rule the Holy Land. Saladin agreed in jest, but Joanna refused to consider the idea!

Late in October other envoys came from Conrad of Monferrat in Tyre. Once again it seemed that the Crusaders were unable to maintain a unified front. Meanwhile there were some skirmishes around Lydda but many Crusaders returned to Acre. King Guy tried to bring them back but was again ignored and only Richard's personal intervention made the troops respond. Richard also faced problems in Cyprus so he sold the island to the Templars. Furthermore Richard was worried about his lands in France now that King Philip Augustus had returned. For his part Saladin heard that his troublesome but admired nephew, Taqi al-Din, had died after making an unauthorized attack on the Muslim ruler of Khilat, worsening Saladin's already tense relationship with the 'Abbasid Caliph in Baghdad.

Negotiations continued through November and Conrad is even said to have offered to break with other Crusader leaders if Saladin were to give him Sidon and Beirut, though he would not fight against Richard. On 11 November Saladin summoned his council to discuss these varying proposals. Most preferred Richard because he would be leaving whereas Conrad would stay and was considered more dangerous. At one point the rival Crusader ambassadors saw each other, though at a distance. Conrad used Balian d'Ibelin as one of his negotiators, and King Richard's poet Ambroise consequently presents him in somewhat unfavourable light:

> Ço fud Balians d'Ibelin
> Qui iert plus faus de gobelin.
> (There went Balian d'Ibelin
> Who was more false than a goblin)

After Saladin again pulled back to the Palestinian highlands at Latrun, the Crusaders occupied Ramla and skirmishing grew more intense. Richard himself was nearly captured near Tal al-Safiya. The king could

not, however, advance towards Jerusalem until his vulnerable supply lines
were protected and it was the failure to do this adequately, rather than the
bad weather, which eventually defeated the Crusaders' advance. But any
assumption that there would be a cessation in hostilities during the winter
failed to appreciate Richard's determination, or the enthusiasm of his
troops. Indeed many of the injured Crusaders recuperating in Jaffa were
so keen to join Richard's advance that they were carried to rejoin the
army, though many were killed by enemy raiders on the road.

On 22 December a large body of reinforcements arrived from Egypt
and camped near Jerusalem. Three days later the Crusaders occupied
Latrun while their advance guard took Bayt Nuba. It was bitterly cold
and the rain fell in torrents, turning the roads and tracks to mud. On 28
December the Crusader advance resumed, with the Muslims harassing
them where they could. Morale was still high amongst ordinary
Crusaders, but those who knew the country warned Richard that he
risked being cut off if he pressed on. Amongst those who advised King
Richard against advancing further were the Grand Masters of the
Templars and Hospitallers. Amongst those most keen on continuing
were the French Crusaders under Hugues of Burgundy.

On 8 January, Richard ordered a retreat to the coastal plain. Some
modern military historians have suggested that Saladin's position was now
so weak that he could not have saved Jerusalem. Certainly Pope Celestine
was not impressed by Richard's performance, having promised so much
yet delivered so little. Richard had also lost the confidence of much of the
army, not only the French and even some of his own followers. Realizing
he had to revive the army's morale, Richard convinced the other senior

leaders that Ascalon should be taken and refortified. This was done with relative ease and morale did indeed revive, with many of the French rejoining Richard.

February saw quarrels break out again and there was fighting in Acre between the Genoese who favoured Conrad and the Pisans who still supported King Guy. Meanwhile, Richard proposed to move to Egypt but received little support. For his part, Saladin ordered his army to mobilize in the Jazira and northern Iraq while water sources around Jerusalem were polluted or filled. Negotiations now resumed again, but Ascalon had beome a major stumbling block to any agreement between King Richard and Saladin. In early April the Prior of Hereford arrived from England, begging Richard to come home because the king's brother John was usurping power, so Richard summoned a council of leaders and demanded that the question of the Crown of Jerusalem be settled urgently. To his surprise, everyone wanted Conrad of Monferrat to replace Guy de Lusignan as king.

It seemed as if the main source of friction within Crusader ranks was settled, but on 28 April Conrad was murdered, almost certainly in retaliation for piracy by Conrad's ships against a merchant vessel owned by the Isma'ilis of northern Syria. The people of Tyre now demanded that Henry of Champagne marry Conrad's widow Isabella and become 'King of Jerusalem' while Guy was encouraged to buy the troublesome island of Cyprus from the Templars.

TOP LEFT **King Richard's conquest of Cyprus marked the end of Byzantine rule. This wall painting of the Betrayal of Christ was made just a few years later.** (*In situ* **Church of Agios Neophytos, Enkleistra**)

TOP RIGHT **King Richard is said to have caught a distant glimpse of Jerusalem while out hunting during his failed attempt to retake the Holy City. (Author's photograph)**

Meanwhile, Saladin was also facing political problems in the Jazira region beyond the river Euphrates. Rumours of these difficulties reached the Crusader camp, and King Richard abandoned his almost completed peace deal with Saladin. Instead he launched a sudden assault on Darum, on the frontier with Egypt. The day before Darum fell, al-Adil set off in hope of settling the Jazira problem but further weakened Saladin's position in Jerusalem; however, Richard now fell ill. Nevertheless the Crusaders prepared another major push towards Jerusalem. On 11 June they again reached Bayt Nuba where they halted for a month and it was during this period that King Richard suddenly caught sight of Jerusalem while pursuing some of Saladin's scouts near Imwas.

King Richard now learned that a large caravan was on its way from Egypt, via al-Arish and Beersheba towards Hebron and Jerusalem. On 22 June he left camp with a large force and, fearing for the caravan, Saladin sent a small detachment to inform its commander, al-Adil's half-brother Falak al-Din. Unfortunately this warning was not followed and on 23 June Richard seized merchandise, abundant quantities of food and, perhaps more importantly, thousands of camels and baggage horses. Interestingly enough, the military author al-Harawi was with this caravan and subsequently used the event as an example of the kind of mistakes that could be made.[17]

On 1 July Saladin summoned his commanders in Jerusalem to discuss what was now a very serious situation. Although the *amirs* pledged their loyalty, many of their troops feared that a siege of Jerusalem would end like Acre, with the city falling and its defenders being massacred. There was also tension between Turks and Kurds, so

Saladin handed the city over to Bahram Shah, the governor of Baalbek, and took command of the army in the hills outside Jerusalem. Meanwhile al-Afdal had finally returned with his army and other reinforcements were on their way.

The scene seemed set for a major showdown but on the evening of 3 July Izz al-Din Jurdik, in command of the advance guard, reported that the Crusaders had left their camp but then returned to it. In fact there were disagreements again within the Crusader army between Richard who wanted to withdraw and the French who wanted to attack Jerusalem. Next day Saladin was told that the Crusaders were retreating. Hardly daring to believe such news, he rode to watch their withdrawal from Bayt Nuba towards Ramla.

Less than a week later Richard sent a message to Saladin requesting negotiations. The talking continued on and off, while Saladin's position gradually became stronger with the arrival of yet more reinforcements. The main sticking point was the fate of Ascalon whereas Jerusalem no longer seemed to have been a major issue. On 27 July Saladin tried to seize Jaffa while Richard was in Acre, planning to attack Beirut. The town fell but the citadel held out. Richard hurried back by sea and, with the personal courage and prowess for which he was famous, drove back Saladin's more numerous troops on 31 July.

August saw negotiations resume in earnest, though Ascalon remained a sticking point. The last serious fighting was on 4 August when Saladin attempted another assault on Jaffa. Although he knew Richard was there, he also knew the Crusaders were few in number and had even fewer horses. Several assaults by Muslim cavalry, including elite troops, were defeated. Some military historians have read a great deal into the tactics adopted by Richard during this sudden attack, where the front rank of Crusader soldiers knelt behind their shields and used their spears as pikes. Behind them stood archers and crossbowmen, the latter working in pairs, each pair comprising a shooter and loader. The Crusaders may also have erected a wooden barricade. Inside this formation were a few mounted knights. However, this infantry array was not a new idea in the Islamic World. It was probably also known in northern Italy and Richard's success largely reflected his deployment of 400 Pisan and Genoese crossbowmen.

Negotiations resumed yet again. By late August Richard was seriously ill while Saladin's health was also failing. The Crusader army was exhausted and widely demoralized; Saladin's army was similarly too weak and too short of munitions to take advantage. On 28 August Saladin sent what most chroniclers agree was his final offer, and on 1 September the terms of a prolonged truce were drawn up. Richard signed the following day, Saladin's representatives the day after. The armies now began to fraternize and many Crusaders completed their pilgrimage to Jerusalem, escorted by Muslim troops, though Richard did not go. On 10 September most of Saladin's troops went home. Nearly three weeks later Queen Berengaria and Queen Joanna set sail from Acre, King Richard following on 9 October. The Third Crusade was over.

16 M.C. Lyons & D.E.P. Jackson, *Saladin: The politics of the Holy War*, Cambridge (1982), p.338.
17 Al, Harawi, op. cit., p.230.

THE BATTLEFIELD TODAY

The initial operations around Tyre (Sur), Beaufort castle, and King Guy's advance from Tyre to besiege Acre took place within the southernmost part of Lebanon which has been open to visitors since the withdrawal of Israeli troops several years ago. However, it will probably be some time before the frontier between Lebanon and Israel is opened. Once the Third Crusade itself reached the Middle Eastern mainland, almost all its military operations took place within Israel proper, with minor excursions into what are currently the occupied Palestinian territories.

The first major operation was the siege of Acre which involved the city and its immediate surroundings (see Campaign 154: *The Fall of Acre 1286–1291* for a full description of this area), plus the coastal plain of Galilee. The Crusader army's subsequent march along the coast, shadowed by Saladin's army, took the combatants down the narrow waist of Israel between the Mediterranean coast and the Palestinian West Bank. This part of Israel is densely populated with good roads and public transport, but is also highly industrialized. As a result much of the landscape has changed considerably since the 12th century. Few of the original villages remain while many of the medieval coastal towns now exist only as archaeological sites, having been replaced by Israeli 'new towns'. Though not particularly attractive, the latter have adequate if rather expensive accommodation.

The presence of closed military zones and strategic industrial sites means that only parts of the Crusaders' line of march can be followed. Nevertheless the existence of national parks such as the Sharon Beach Nature Reserve offer an insight into the difficulties faced by tired, hungry and overburdened troops as they struggled along under frequent enemy attack. The nature reserve actually lies at the northern end of the battlefield of Arsuf and any serious student should visit it. Forests dotted Palestine until the early 20th century, when huge swathes were cut down to provide timber for the new Ottoman Turkish railway system. During the second half of the 20th century the Israeli government, like others in the Middle East, tried to replace them, but the newly wooded areas are not the same in appearance as the medieval forests, and even the species of trees

Once King Richard took control of Jaffa, the Crusaders used it as a base from which they unsuccessfully tried to retake Jerusalem. (Author's photograph)

Ramla on the coastal plain of Palestine was a major hub of medieval communications and had reliable water supplies in the form of the 'Cistern of St. Helena', built for the Caliph Harun al-Rashid in AD 789. (Author's photograph)

are different. To form an impression of the terrain into which Saladin's troops withdrew during the course of the battle of Arsuf, the visitor has to go to one of relatively few surviving 'natural forests'. One of the most beautiful is near Yoqne-Am on the road from the coastal plain to the Jezreel valley, the same road that Saladin's army took after the loss of Acre.

It is important for visitors who hire self-drive cars and leave the tourist routes to understand that the normal tourist maps are not entirely accurate. Centres of habitation which appear on such maps, be they 'Zionist settlements' or 'Arab villages', are normally those which have official recognition. Closer inspection of more detailed maps show other unnamed habitations and care should be taken when visiting these as some are so-called 'illegal' Arab hamlets. They may have been there long before the foundation of the state of Israel, or may have been established by Palestinians evicted from their homes in 1948 but who nevertheless remained within the territory that became Israel. Such hamlets are normally small, lack electricity, sewage services and sometimes even educational facilities while their inhabitants can be defensive if not overtly paranoid, so visitors who speak neither Arabic nor Hebrew should treat them with care and sensitivity.

Since the recent relocation of an Israeli munitions factory, the medieval city of Arsuf has been partially opened to visitors. Unfortunately much of the ground, especially outside the walls of the fortified city, is still polluted by toxic chemicals. Consequently, part of the ground over which Richard's and Saladin's troops fought remains out of bounds. Immediately south of Arsuf, where the Crusaders made camp after the battle, lies the upmarket and entirely modern Israeli town of Herzliyya whose hotels, restaurants and vibrant night life make an excellent base from which to explore those parts of the Arsuf battlefield which are accessible.

The next major location on the Crusaders' march was Jaffa, which also featured prominently in Saladin's subsequent attempts to defeat King Richard. This is now a picturesque suburb and artists' colony within greater Tel Aviv. Its appearance and architecture are Arab while its population is largely Israeli–Jewish. As a result present-day Jaffa has an unreal and almost 'Disney World' air about it. A major difficulty in 'walking the ground' of this part of the Third Crusade is that most places have either been replaced by new Israeli settlements or towns, or have been obliterated entirely, or have disappeared beneath factories or airfields. The majority have also changed their name.

Ramla, or that part now called Old Ramla, is an exception and has retained much of its original Arab population. It is worth a visit, though it cannot in all justice be described as beautiful. It is easier to identify locations and traditional routes when following the Crusaders' unsuccessful marches towards Jerusalem, but even here there are problems. For example, the strategic village of Emmeus (Amwas) was bulldozed out of existence in late 1967. Latrun was also obliterated, though the modern French monastery and the ruins of a small Crusader castle can still be seen.

The latter part of the Third Crusade saw both sides campaigning across a large area of what are now southern Israel, the south-western corner of the Palestinian West Bank and the Gaza Strip. Almost all the fighting, as opposed to manoeuvring, took place on the coast and in the Judean foothills which now largely lie almost entirely within Israel proper. By hiring a car, the battlefield tourist can follow the routes taken by Richard, by Saladin and by their subordinate commanders. The countryside is scenic, the ex-Palestinian villages with their ruined mosques and some surviving minarets are occasionally beautiful, if rather sad, and some of the Israeli settlements have a quiet charm.

That leaves the Gaza Strip which is currently in no state to welcome visitors, though its tourist potential is greater than might first appear. The most important site associated with the Third Crusade within the Strip is Darom; normally identified as present-day Dayr al-Ballah. Like most other places in the Gaza Strip, the old village is now accompanied by a large refugee camp which does not have ordinary facilities for visitors; at least not for tourists. However, writing as one who has visited several such Palestinian refugee camps, I can state that the people are hugely friendly, welcoming and almost absurdly generous with what little they have, especially when it comes to offering their guest a meal. All that they expect in return is courtesy, a friendly ear and respect.

BIBLIOGRAPHY

Abu Shama, 'Kitab al-Rawdatayn' in *Recueil des Historiens des Croisades: Historiens Orientaux*, IV & V, Paris (1898)

Abu'l-Fida, 'Résumé de l'histoire des Croisades, tiré des Annales d'Abou'l-Fedâ' in *Recueil des Historiens des Croisades: Historiens Orientaux*, I, Paris (1872)

Ambroise (ed. & tr. M. Ailes & M. Barber), *The History of the Holy War: Ambroise's Estoire de la Guerre Sainte*, Woodbridge (2003)

Anon. (ed. H.J. Nicholson), *The Chronicle of the Third Crusade: The Itinerarium Peregrinorum et Gesta Regis Ricardi*, Aldershot (2001)

Anon. (ed. R.C. Johnston), *The Crusade and Death of Richard I: Anglo-Norman Texts XVII*, Oxford (1961)

Archer, T.A. (ed.), *The Crusade of Richard I: 1189–92*, English History by Contemporary Writers, 5, London (1889)

Audouin, E., *Essai sur l'Armée Royale au Temps de Philippe Auguste*, Paris (1913)

Azhari, T.K. el-, 'The office of the Atabeg in Syria under the Nurids and the Ayyubids' in *Al-Masaq*, 11, (1999), pp.47–66

Baha' al-Din Ibn Shaddad (tr. D.S. Richards), *The Rare and Excellent History of Saladin*, Aldershot (2002)

Bradbury, J., *Philip Augustus: King of France 1180–1223*, London (1997)

Brand, C.M., 'The Byzantines and Saladin, 1185–1192: Opponents of the Third Crusade' in *Speculum*, XXXVII, (1962), pp.167–181

Contamine, P., 'L'Armée de Philippe Auguste' in R-H. Bautier (ed.), *La France de Philippe Auguste*, Paris (1982), pp.577–593

Edbury, P.W., *The Conquest of Jerusalem and the Third Crusade: Sources in Translation*, Aldershot (1996)

Edbury, P.W., *The Kingdom of Cyprus and the Crusades 1191–1374*, Cambridge (1991)

Edde, A-M., 'Kurdes et Turcs dans l'Armée Ayyoubide de Syrie du Nord' in Y. Lev (ed.), *War and Society in the Eastern Mediterranean, 7th–15th Centuries*, Leiden (1996), pp.225–236

Edde, A-M., 'Quelques institutions militaires ayyoubide' in U. Vermeulen & D. De Smet (eds.), *Egypt and Syria in the Fatimid, Ayyubid and Mamluk Eras*, Leuven (1995), pp.163–174

Ehrenkreutz, A.S., 'The Place of Saladin in the Naval History of the Mediterranean Sea in the Middle Ages' in *Journal of American Oriental Studies*, LXXV, (1955), pp.100–116

Ehrenkreutz, A.S., *Saladin*, New York (1972)

Eickhoff, E., 'Friedrich Barbarossa im Orient: Istanbuler Mitteilungen', *Beiheft 17*, Tübingen (1977)

Elbeheiry, S., *Les Institutions de l'Egypte au Temps des Ayyubides*, Lille (1972)

Evans, M., 'A far from aristocratic affair: Poor and non-combatant crusaders from the Midlands, c.1160–c.1300' in *Midland History*, XXXI, (1996)

Flori, J., *Richard Coeur de Lion, le roi-chevalier*, Collection 'Biographie', Paris (1999)

France, J., 'Crusading warfare and its adaptation to Eastern conditions in the twelfth century' in *Mediterranean Historical Review*, 15, (2000), pp.49–66

France, J., *Western Warfare in the Age of the Crusades 1000–1300*, New York (1999)

Gibb, H.A.R., 'The Arabic Sources for the Life of Saladin' in *Speculum*, XXV, (1950), pp.58–74

Gibb, H.A.R., 'The Armies of Saladin' in *Cahiers d'Histoire Egyptienne*, III, (1951), pp.304–320

Gibb, H.A.R., *The Life of Saladin*, Oxford (1973)

Gillingham, J., 'Richard I and the Science of War in the Middle Ages' in J. Gillingham & J.C. Holt (eds.), *War and Government in the Middle Ages: Essays in Honour of J.O. Prestwich*, Cambridge (1984), pp.78–91

Gillingham, J., *Richard Coeur de Lion: Kingship, Chivalry and War in the Twelfth Century*, London (1994)

Gillingham, J., *Richard the Lionheart*, London (1978)

Gore, T.L., *The Campaigns of Saladin: Hattin and Arsuf 1187 and 1193 AD*, New York (1991)

Guillaume le Breton (ed. F. Delaborde), 'Gesta Philippi Augusti' in *Oeuvres de Rigord et de Guillaume le Breton*, tome 1, Paris (1882)

Guillaume le Breton (ed. F. Delaborde), 'Philillidos' in *Oeuvres de Rigord et de Guillaume le Breton*, tome 2, Paris (1885)

Hamblin, W.J., 'Saladin and Muslim Military Theory' in B.Z. Kedar (ed.), *The Horns of Hattin*, London (1992), pp.228–238

Hiestand, R., 'Kingship and Crusade in C12th Germany' in A. Haverkamp (ed.), *England and Germany in the High Middle Ages*, Oxford (1996), pp.235–265

Holt, P.M., 'Saladin and his admirers…' *Bulletin of the School of Oriental and African Studies*, XLVI, (1983), pp.235–239

Ibish, Y. (ed.), *Saladin: Studies in Islamic History*, Beirut (1972)

Ibn al-Athir, 'Extrait de la Chronique intitulée Kamel Altevarykh' in *Recueil des Historiens des Croisades: Historiens Orientaux*, I, Paris (1872)

Ibn Shaddad (tr. D.S. Richards), *The Rare and Excellent History of Saladin*, Aldershot (2001)

Imad al-Din al-Katib al-Isfahani (tr. H. Massè), *Conquête de la Syrie et de la Palestine par Saladin*, Paris (1972)

Kedar, B.Z., 'A Western Survey of Saladin's Forces at the Siege of Acre' in B.Z. Kedar (et al eds.), *Montjoie: Studies in Crusade History in Honour of Hans Eberhard Mayer*, Aldershot (1997), pp.113–122

La Monte, J.L., 'Taki ed Din, Prince of Hama,' in *The Moslem World*, XXXI, (1941), pp.149–160

Lev, Y., *Saladin in Egypt*, Leiden (1998)

Lewis, B., 'Saladin and the Assassins' in *Bulletin of the School of Oriental and African Studies*, 15, (1952), pp.239–245

Ligato, G., 'Corrado di Monferrato e la corte di Saladino…,' in G.S. Rondinini (ed.), *Il Monferrato: crocevia politico, economico e culturale tra Mediterraneo e Europa*, Ponzone (2000), pp.111–140

Ligato, G., 'Saladino e i prigioneri di guerra' in G. Cipollone (ed.), *La liberazione dei 'captivi' tra Cristianita e Islam*, Vatican (2000), pp.649–654

Lonchambon, C. (ed.), *L'Aquitaine Ducale: Histoire Médiévale*, Hors Série No. 7, Apt (2004)

Lyons, M.C., & D.E.P. Jackson, *Saladin, The Politics of the Holy War*, Cambridge (1982)

Markowski, M., 'Richard Lionheart: bad king, bad crusader?' in *Journal of Medieval History*, 23 (1997) pp.351–365

Marshall, C.J., 'The Use of the Charge in Battle in the East, 1192–1291,' in *Historical Research*, LXIII, (1990), pp.221–226

Ménard, P., 'Les combattants en Terre Sainte au temps de Saladin et de Richard Coeur de Lion' in J. Paviot & J. Verger (eds.), *Guerre, pouvoir et noblesse au Moyen Age: Mélanges en l'honneur de Philippe Contamine*, Paris (2000), pp.503–511

Mouton, J-M., *Saladin: le sultan chevalier*, Paris (2001)

Munz, P., *Frederick Barbarossa. A Study in Medieval Politics*, London (1969)

Newby, P., *Saladin and his Time* (1983)

Nicholson, H., 'Women on the Third Crusade' in *Journal of Medieval History*, XXIII, (1997), pp.335–349

Nicolaou-Konnari, A., 'The Conquest of Cyprus by Richard the Lionheart and its aftermath' in *Epitirida tou Kentrou Epistimonikon Evrenon*, 26, Nicosia (2000), pp.25–123

Otto of Friesing (tr. C.C. Mierow), *The Deeds of Frederick Barbarossa* (1953)

Pacaut, M., *Frederick Barbarossa* (1970)

Paterson, J.F., 'The Battle of Arsuf' in Journal of the Society of Archer Antiquaries, VIII, (1965), pp.22–23

Prestwich, J.O., 'Richard Coeur de Lion: Rex Bellicosus' in J.L. Nelson (ed.), *Richard Coeur de Lion in History and Myth*, London (1992)

Regan, G., Lionhearts, *Saladin and Richard I*, London (1998)

Regan, G., *Saladin and the Fall of Jerusalem*, London (1987)

Rogers, R., *Latin Siege Warfare in the Twelfth Century*, Oxford (1992)

Round, J.H., 'Some English Crusaders of Richard I' in *English Historical Review*, XVIII, (1903)

Salih, A.H., 'Saladins et les Bedouins d'Egypte' in *Rendiconti della Reale Accademia Nazionale dei Lincei* (Cl. Sci. mor. Stor. Filol), Scienze Morali, XXXIV, (1979), pp.349–354

Sayers, J., 'English Charters from the Third Crusade' in D. Greenway (et al. eds.), *Tradition and Change: Essays in Honour of Marjorie Chibnall presented by her friends on the occasion of her seventieth birthday*, Cambridge (1985), pp.195–213

Selcer, R., 'Blondel: The Lionheart's Minstrel' in *Medieval History*, 9, (May 2004), pp.46–55

Selcer, R., 'The Captive King: Richard the Lionheart' in *Medieval History*, 12, (August 2004), pp.28–39

Sibt al-Jawzi, 'Mir'at al-Zaman,' in *Recueil des Historiens des Croisades: Historiens Orientaux*, III, Paris (1884)

Smail, R.C., *Crusading Warfare*, 1097–1193, Oxford (1956)

Tolan, J., 'Mirror of Chivalry: Salah al-Din in the medieval European imagination' in *Images of the Other. Europe and the Muslim World before 1700, Cairo Papers on Social Science*, 19, (1997), pp.7–38

Trotel Costedoat, K., & F.D. Le Claire Arago, 'Philippe Auguste, "un don du Ciel" ' in *Histoire Médiévale*, 37, (Janvier 2003), pp.38–41

Trotel Costedoat, K., 'L'Avancée du Pouvoir Royal sous Philippe Auguste' in *Histoire Médiévale*, 37, (Janvier 2003), pp.42–47

Turner, R.V., & R.R. Heiser, *The Reign of Richard Lionheart: Ruler of the Angevin Empire 1189-1199*, London (2000)

Wolf, G. (ed.), *Friedrich Barbarossa*, Darmstadt (1975)

INDEX

Figures in **bold** refer to illustrations

Acre, siege of 18, 20, 23, 26, 27, **30,** 31, 37, 46–55, 90
al-Adil 21, 35, 58, 71, 74, 80, 81, 83, 87
al-Afdal 21–2, 55, 71, 81, 88
Albigensian Crusades 15
Aleppo 9, **9,** 22, 47
Ambroise 19, **62,** 71, 74–5, 76, 84
Anatolia 43, **43**
Angelus, Emperor Isaac 12, 14, 40, 43
Angevins, the 15, 26
Anglicus, Gilbert 26
Anjou, Count of 15
Antioch 10, 11, 40, 42
Arab Fertile Crescent 9, 36
archers
    Crusaders 25, **25**
    Muslim 26, 35–6, 38
armour
    Crusaders **8, 25,** 25–6, **26, 28, 74**
    Muslim 31, **32, 58**
Arsuf
    battle of 8, **11,** 19, 20, 21, 23, 25, 34–5, 37, 38–9, **58, 59, 63, 66,** 67–82, **70,** 90, 91
    the march to 55–67
Artuqid dynasty 11–12
Ascalon 83, **84, 85,** 86, 88
Assize of Arms **26**
Atabegs 11, 21
al-Athir, Ibn 74, 79–80, 80
Austria, Duke of 47, **50,** 54, **88**
Avesnes, James d' 20, 67, 80
Awja River 81
Ayaz the Tall 59, **62**
Ayyubids, the 20, 32
al-Aziz 20–1

Baalbek 21
Baghras 40
Bahram Shah 88
Baldwin, Archbishop 46
Barbarossa, Emperor Frederick 12, 14, 18, 27–9, **29, 42,** 42–3, **43, 44,** 46
Barres, William de 80
Bayt Nuba 85, 87, 88
Beaufort, castle of 10, 23, 42, 46

Bedouin tribes 32–3, 35, 36, 66, 75
Belvoir, siege of 40
Bennett, Matthew 18, 37
Berbers, the 32
Berengaria, Queen 89
Blois, Count of 27
Brabançones 25
Bremen 46
Bulgaria 12, 43
Burgundy, Duke of 18–19, 27, 55, 58, 85
Byzantine Empire 7, 8, 11, 12, 14, 37, 43, 51

Caesarea **54,** 58, 59, **59**
campaign origins 7–17
Carpenter, D. 18
Catulus, Roger Malus 26
Caymont 55, 58
Celestine, Pope 85
Champagne, Henry of 19–20, 27, 46, 67, 86
Christian commanders 18–20
chronology 16–17
Clairvaux, Abbot of 55, 76
Clermont, Count of 27
Coeur de Lion see Richard I, King
Cologne 46
communications, inadequacy of 7
Comnenid dynasty 12
Comnenus, Isaac 14, 51
Comnenus, Manuel 14
Constance, Queen of Sicily 46
Constantinople 10, 14
Cottereaux 25
Council of Le Mans 24
crossbows 25, **25,** 27
Crusader armies 24–31
Cyprus 14, 84, **86**

Damascus 9, 10, 21, 23, **29,** 40
Darum 87
Dayr al-Ballah 92
Dayr al-Rabib 66, 92
Destroit, castle of **54**
Didymotikon 43
al-Din, Baha' 23, 31, 33, 55, 59, 66, 71, 74, 75, 78–9, 80, 81
al-Din, Falak 87
al-Din, Imad 22, 80
al-Din, Nur 20

al-Din, Qutb 43
al-Din, Sarim 22–3, 71
al-Din, Taqi 21, 51, **53,** 71, 80, 84
doctors 26–7
Dreux, Count of 27
drugs 9

Edirne 43
Egypt 9, 11, 21, 33, 74, 85, 86
Emmeus 92
European Age of Discovery 42

Fatimid Caliphal Palace **22, 40**
Feoda Campanie 27
'l-Fida, Abu 79
field hospitals 26–7
finance 26, 27, 28, 29
Flanders, Count Philippe of 27
Flemings 25
France 14–15, 27, 84
Frisia 46

Garnier de Naples 71
Gaza Strip 92
Genoa 7, **7,** 30
Geoffrey de Lusignan 20, 58, 67, 83
Gerard de Rideford 67
Germany 14, 27–9, **29,** 42–6
    ministeriales 24, 29
ghulams 32
Glanvill **26**
Gloucester, Sheriff of 27
Göksu River **44,** 46
Guy, King of Jerusalem 10, 19, 20, 46, 55, 67, 84, 86, 90

Haifa **53**
Haj pilgrim caravans 40
Hakkari tribe 33
Hama 79
Hanafi school of Islamic law 9
harafish 35
al-Harawi 31–2, 35, 38–9, 87
Harran 47
hashish, use of 9
Hattin, battle of 10, 21, 83
Hebron 87
Henry II, King 15, **26,** 42, 46
Henry III, Count of Troyes 19–20, 27, 46, 67, 86

95

Hereford, Prior of 86
Herzliyya 91
Hiestand, R. 29
Historia de expeditione Frederici imperatoris 29
Hospitallers, the 9, 22, **30**, 31, 67, 71, 75–6, 78, 85
hospitals 26–7
Hugues III, Duke of Burgundy 18–19, 27, 55, 58, 85

Ibelin, Balian d' 84
injuries 26–7, 81
Iraq 33, 86
Islamic forces 31–6
Italy 7, 14, 30, **30**
Itinerarium 74–5, 79, 80

Jaffa 37, 38, 83, 85, 88, **90**, 91
Jazira 11
Jerusalem 8, 9, **9**, 10, 19, 31, 42, 55, 83, **83**, 85, 86, **86**, 89
Jews 14
jihad 8
Joanna, Queen of Sicily 83, 89
John, King 15, 86

Keeper of the King's Seal 26
Khirbat-al-Jayus 79
Kilij Arslan II, Sultan 43
Kingdom of Jerusalem *see* Jerusalem
Kipchaq Turks 12
Konya, Sultan of 22, 43, **44**
Kurds 9, 12, 32, 33, **34**, 36, 87

Latrun 83, 84, 92
Law of War, German 29
Leicester, Earl of 26, 78
Leopold, Duke of Austria 47, **50**, 54, **88**
Louis VII, King 15
Lusignan, Geoffrey de 20, 58, 67, 83
Lusignan, Guy de *see* Guy, King of Jerusalem
Lydda 83, 84

Majdal Yaba 58, 81
mamluks 32, 33, 71
Manuel, Byzantine Emperor 9
Merle 58
Military Orders
   Hospitallers, the 9, 22, **30**, 31, 67, 71, 75–6, 78, 85
   Templars, the 31, 67, 71, 84, 85
ministeriales 24, 29
Monferrat, Conrad of 10, 19, 40, 55, 84, 86
Mount Carmel 55, 58
Muslim commanders 20–3

Nahr al-Falik 66, 74
Nahr al-Mafjir 59
Naples, Garnier de 71
Nevers, Count of 27
Niger, Raduphus 28
Nish 42–3
Nubia 11, 32, 35–6
nuzul 38, 74

origins of the campaign 7–17
Ouzes, the 12

Palestine 9, 19, 90
Pecheneg Turks 12
Perche, Count of 27
Philip Augustus, King 14, 15, 18, 19, 24, 27, 42, **46**, 46–7, **50**, 51, 54–5, 84
Pisa 7, 30, 42, 86
Plantagenets, the 15, 26
Plovdiv 43
Poitou, Richard of *see* Richard I, King
Ponthieu, Count of 27
Portugal 42, **42**
Principality of Antioch *see* Antioch
prisoners **9**, 54, 55
Puintel, William 27

Qalaat al-Gindi fortress **11**

Ramla 83, 84, 88, 91–2
Raymond, Count of Tripoli 10
Renaud of Sidon 10
Richard I, King **11**, 14, 15, 18, **18**, 19, 42, **46**
   aftermath 83–9
   the battle of Arsuf **70**, 74–82
   his forces 24, 27
   his plan 37–8
   the march to Arsuf 58, 66–7
   the siege of Acre 46–7, **47**, **50**, 51, 54–5
Ridefort, Gerard de 67
Robert de Sablé 67
Rum, Sultan of 14, 43

Sablé, Robert de 67
sabres **76**
Safad 40
Saffuriya 22
Saladin **7**, 8, 9, **9**, 10–12, 14, 19, 20–1, 37, 41, 42, **42**
   the battle of Arsuf **70**, 71, 74–82, 83–9
   coins depicting **12**
   Fatimid Caliphal Palace **22**
   his forces 31–6
   his plan 38–9

the march to Arsuf 55, 58–9, 66–7
the siege of Acre 46, 47, 51
Salisbury, Bishop of 26
Samsat 22
Sancerre, Count of 27
Saphadin 21
scutage 26
Serbia 12
Shama, Abu 79, 80
Sharon Beach Nature Reserve 90
al-Shayzari 31
Shi'a Muslims 9
Sicily 14, 30, 46
Sidon 10
Silves 42, **42**
spearmen 25
Sudan 11
Sunni Muslims 9
Swabia, Duke Frederick of 29, 47
Syria 33, 35, 40, 79

Tal al-Safiya 84
Tancred, King of Sicily 46–7
al-Tarsusi 31
al-Tawil, Ayaz 59, **62**
Tel Aviv 91
Templar church, Cressac **6**
Templars, the 31, 67, 71, 84, 85
Thuringia 46
Tiberius 22
Torron, Humphrey of 83
Toulouse, Count of 27
trade, expansion of 7
Tripoli 10, 40, 42
Tripoli, Count Raymond of 10
Turks 9, 12, 32, **32**, **35**, 36, **44**, **63**, 87
Tyre 10, 21, 40, 42, 55, 86, 90

Vadum Yaqub 81
Venice 7
Vézelay, France 46, **46**
Vlachs, the 12

Wallachia 12
weapons
   Crusaders 25, **25**, 27
   Muslim 26, **62**, **76**
William de Barres 80
William I, Earl of Derby 26
William II, King of Sicily 42, 46
women, ban on 24
writers, military 31

Yemen 11
Yoqne-Am 91

Zangids, the 11
Zarqa River 59

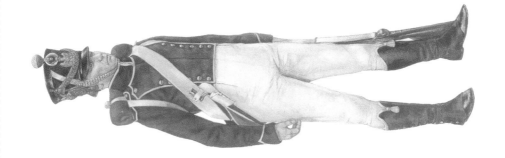

OSPREY
PUBLISHING

FIND OUT MORE ABOUT OSPREY

❏ Please send me the latest listing of Osprey's publications

❏ I would like to subscribe to Osprey's e-mail newsletter

Title / rank

Name

Address

City / county

Postcode / zip   state / country

e-mail

CAM

I am interested in:

❏ Ancient world
❏ Medieval world
❏ 16th century
❏ 17th century
❏ 18th century
❏ Napoleonic
❏ 19th century

❏ American Civil War
❏ World War 1
❏ World War 2
❏ Modern warfare
❏ Military aviation
❏ Naval warfare

Please send to:

North America:
Osprey Direct , 2427 Bond Street, University Park, IL 60466, USA

UK, Europe and rest of world:
Osprey Direct UK, P.O. Box 140, Wellingborough, Northants, NN8 2FA, United Kingdom

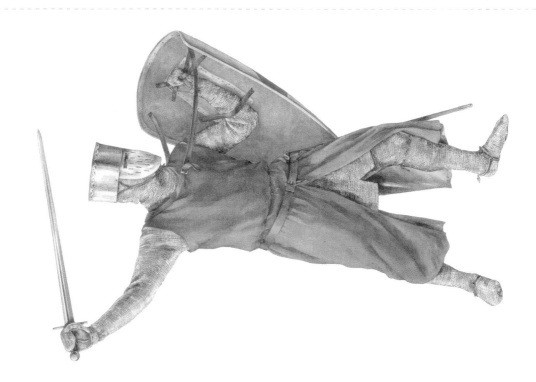

www.ospreypublishing.com

call our telephone hotline
for a free information pack

USA & Canada: 1-800-826-6600
UK, Europe and rest of world call:
+44 (0) 1933 443 863

Young Guardsman
Figure taken from *Warrior 22:
Imperial Guardsman 1799–1815*
Published by Osprey
Illustrated by Richard Hook

Knight, c.1190
Figure taken from *Warrior 1: Norman Knight 950–1204 AD*
Published by Osprey
Illustrated by Christa Hook

POSTCARD